I0426511

101 Fiction Writing Tips

A selection of 101writing tips gained by experience and designed to provide the fiction writer with a useful reference.

By
QUENTIN COPE

MECURIAN BOOKS

https://mecurianbooks.webnode.com

COPYRIGHT & DISCLAIMER

CONTENTS

:Introduction:

Introduction

Fiction writing is thought by many potential authors and writers to be the most popular published genre and therefore perhaps the best to be aiming at when considering a writing career. I started out writing technical manuals and business management publications for limited circulation and struggled to publish my first novel in 1988. The experience of that first encounter with the traditional book publishing circus put me off to such an extent I did not begin to write another novel for more than twenty years. Things have changed dramatically in the publishing world since then with the advent of the Internet and a myriad of good self-publishing routes. Current best estimates are that the market for published books will grow exponentially year on year. Unfortunately, it's difficult to get two knowledgeable individuals to agree on the figures involved and therefore I'm not going to make an uninformed attempt here. However, one reasonably sound statistic is the percentage of fiction and non-fiction publications now produced annually in the English language. The current estimates are around 30% for fiction and 70% for non-fiction.

So, the lesson to learn there then is you may stand a considerably better chance putting together a book of your grandmother's best apple pie secrets than attempting the daunting task of coming face to face with the prospect of writing a novel ... a work of fiction ... a work of fantasy, a work that will need to find a particular audience. The question has always been, and will continue to be ... 'How will someone read your book ... if they don't know it's out there?'

This one hundred and twenty page book is not an answer to that quandary and neither does it offer any form of guarantee to the potential novelist. What is does provide however, is a list of 101 tips of advice and reference to the 'hungry' individual who simply wants' to 'get on with the job!' These offerings are provided from experience of both the self-publishing and traditional publishing routes with advice aimed specifically toward the EBook and Paperback production process.

If, after reading this book, you decide to literally 'put pen to paper' and start that novel ... the one we are told is in all of us, or pick up that dusty manuscript, the one you put safely away some years ago because you 'simply didn't have the time'... then perhaps these few words will have done their job. If the words written here in some way give you a push forward, enabling you to put down that now slightly warm glass of Chardonnay and hit the keyboard once again ... then I can leave your company with a smile on my face.

Finally, as the reader, you should be aware this little

25,000 word book of tips is *not* an instruction manual and therefore does not present lot's of detailed advice in some sort of 'How To' format. If this is what you are looking for, then you may possibly be disappointed. '101 Fiction Writing Tips' is written with the intention of affording you, the potential writer of fantastic fiction, with a series of comfortable statements and explanations written in a language that is easy to understand. Hopefully, some or much of it will provide you with a certain level of help along with answers to questions that could have been hanging around in your mind for a considerable time. The aim is to hopefully provide the single, concise source of assistance you may just have been looking for to further energize you in the pursuit of your fiction writing projects.

Good Luck …

Part 1:
Be Organized

Being organized is the single most important factor in producing a well written, well edited novel or work of fiction, and one that is not simply abandoned on page twenty nine. Many people unfortunately find it difficult to 'get organized' in order to write down the first few paragraphs of their potential best seller. Doing so is all about discipline and starting as you mean to go on. This is the very first step on the road to achieving your goal of perhaps becoming a professional writer, so it's important to make sure you don't lose your footing on the very first rung of a necessarily long ladder.

******

Tip 01: Create a Title Folder:

If you already are an organized person, please bear with me because there are many out there who are not, and maybe I don't need to tell you this but to 'get going' ... the very first thing you really need to do is create a new folder on your PC specifically for your intended manuscript. This is what I do for every writing project. It's too easy to simply throw a 'Word' document on to your hard drive somewhere

… and then days later struggle to find it. So give your project substance right from the very first 'go' by placing everything to do with the project in one single folder. This sounds so ridiculously simple you may well be having a small chuckle to yourself. But make no mistake, much valuable and frustrating time is spent by many potentially great writers trying to find a file they've forgotten the name of, on a stubborn PC that simply refuses to release it. It happens far too often. So, give your folder a title, hopefully the working title of the book itself, or simply 'My Book'. Whatever you do, 'give it a title' as this will focus your thoughts every time you open this folder and keep the storyline in the very forefront of your thinking. Again, you may somehow feel this is teaching a 'grandmother to suck eggs' … but you would be surprised at how many writers ignore this very basic first step to being organized … and end up in a mess!

Tip 02: Create Subject Folders:

Creating subject folders; a simple thing to remember but something often ignored. The 'Title' folder will contain other sub-folders as your needs reveal themselves, but you could well give consideration to starting with the following: *Manuscript, Research, Sketch, Images, Maps, Downloads and Character Profiles.* The file contents of each subject folder will hopefully be self explanatory but the title 'Sketch' may be a new one to you. There is more on this subject later.

Tip 03: Create Hard Copy Folders:

For the 'non-PC' writer or typewriter specialist, you will obviously need to create real, hold-'em-in-your-hand files, and ones that will become progressively thicker as the project evolves. When your writing project begins to develop, it's a good idea to keep them 'near' you … you will refer to them regularly. This is the way I used to manage my writing projects in the 70's and 80's BC (Before Computers) and I feel sure there are not many pen and paper writers left out there now. However, I do know of one very famous thriller writer who still puts down his work on paper with a manual typewriter and employs someone to 'organize' the manuscript on a PC. So if you are one of those who would prefer to write in hard copy, please do so but also make every effort you can to be 'organized'!

Part 2:
Your Subject

For Fiction writers, the subject material for your new novel could be any one of the following genre: *Action & Adventure: Classics: Fantasy: General Fiction: Literary Fiction: Mystery: Romance: Suspense & Thrillers: Science Fiction: Western: Contemporary and Historical Fiction.* There are of course many more categories and genres available to slot your new work in to and you will have to make up your mind which one suits your cause best; but once you have chosen *one*, you are on your way. All of my novels fall generally in the 'Action & Adventure' category or 'Thrillers'. However, I have to admit that one or two started out in my mind originally as being in one genre … and ended up in another. Read on…

******

Tip 04: How Much Fact in Your Fiction?

Yes, it's true. Many manuscripts in the writing start out as placed in one genre and end up in another. That's a fact! How is that possible? Well, a good example could be when you set out to write an Action & Adventure work of fiction. Without necessarily being aware of it, you find, halfway through the manuscript, you have drifted toward writing about a real person ... one that maybe you have known in the dim and distant past. You end up actually putting down on the written page, a synopsis of the life of a humorous, ebullient and adventurous character you knew well in a previous part of your life. So, my asking the question about 'how much fact is in your fiction?' highlights a common situation. Beware of slipping into this trap ... it happens all too often!

Tip 05: Select A Subject:

So the first big decision to contemplate is how to place your story; in what theatre of events, in what country and what language. By now, the story line may be so strong with you it will be literally fighting to beat a path out of your brain. You will of course have given much thought to the detailed setting, the period and the characters and now you want to write chapter one! That's great. You know how to start it ... but is there something you may have forgotten?

Tip 06: Consider An Age Group:

Having a story in mind and knowing the genre within which it will be placed, means you are nearly there. The final consideration is to keep in mind the 'age group' you will be writing for. If you are keen to produce a 'teen romp' for example, you will obviously need to communicate with your reader in a totally different manner from those in a 40 to 50 age group. If your setting is far in the future, as in Sci-Fi, or in some fantasy land or other, you can more or less say what you like ... without it being questioned. However, if you are presenting your story line set in the 80's or 90's to a fifty year old ... someone who actually lived through those years ... you will need to be accurate in your research of the period, as this reader will possibly have a much better grasp than you of *what was* and *was not* possible during those years. Try not to make the mistake of having your character driving a car that hadn't been produced yet. You are bound to lose some credibility ... and someone will write and tell you where you've gone wrong!

Tip 07: The Storyline:

A fiction writer is simply a 'story teller' who will often admit that many of the characters, some of the places and often an embellished set of events, have been gathered together from real memories, of real people, in real situations. Therefore, as a fiction writer, it's a good idea to make sure your characters are as unrecognizable as sensibly possible by the real person, if they are still alive, especially where character names are concerned. Make sure *your* story line is in fact *'yours'*, is *'genuine'* and not an amalgam of many stories you have read in the past. If you don't, you may find it an easy start ... but take my word for it, such a project will be a very difficult finish!

Tip 08: The Setting Research Plan:

When writing fiction, with a scenario in the past or present, then it's most useful to make sure everything researchable is indeed, well researched. From makes of cars driven, to types of watches consulted … from the ring of a particular telephone to the name of the hotel your character stayed in. It's essential to good fiction writing to make sure, that within the setting of your manuscript, the scenery and props are all seen to be reality and match the fiction scenario you have conjured up. You will be painting a picture, a background, a stage upon which to place your characters … and I'm sure you may have heard it all before, but it *is* important. If you strive to do your research well, this will give you confidence as the storyline progresses and you move your characters around the setting.

Tip 09: The Character Research Plan:

The characters making up the meat of your storyline are probably so well formed in your head you could perhaps feel you don't need to do anything, other than simply throw their names down on the page. In your own world of fiction, that's absolutely fine. However, this process allows the possibility of you writing some of your characters in to roles, within the storyline, they are not equipped to handle. Having a seventy year old ex truck driver running a three minute mile, then jumping a twelve foot wide stream, to escape the clutches of the villain on a bicycle moving at twenty miles an hour, will raise eyebrows amongst some of your more 'picky' readers ... and may even prompt them to put your beautifully written work down. The simple answer? ... make sure you have written a full 'Bio' for each of your characters and as you write, you will often see so much more, or so much less in them than you originally thought. No doubt, you have probably heard this before, but it's always a really good idea to try and ensure your characters, and the situations they find themselves in, are reasonable. I have always held dear to the thought that a 'poets license' is for poets ... and not for good fiction writers.

Tip 10: The Sketch:

The benefits of producing a detailed sketch as a preliminary to your manuscript may, by now be coming obvious, in that during the process, you will naturally tend to organize your thoughts and construct your characters within a plot. If you have a theme in mind, this will help you to deliver exactly what you *plan* to deliver, and when dealing with a complex plot and a cast of many characters, this will assist greatly in eliminating scenario failures. In general, there are three things you might want to outline in your sketch: back-story, characters, and plot. You may also want to make sure you fully iron out the plot and story-line in fine detail especially if your work veers toward the convoluted murder mystery or complex political thriller. (You can find out more about writing a sketch in Part 4)

Tip 11: The Back Story:

For the back-story, it would be a good idea to ensure you don't get carried away. It's easy to do and I have done it myself on several occasions. It's fairly essential for a fiction storyline to have a well developed history, but my advice would be to not get so involved in creating a past that your main character begins to lose sight of the present. If the back-story becomes too cumbersome and detailed, it may well overwhelm the main story you're trying so hard to lay down … and can also be a black hole for some writers. A lot of sci-fi and fantasy is prone to this quite major story-line issue. The action and pace of a good thriller can be slowed down considerably when the back story takes over for a page or two. Some regard a lively back story to be essential to the main plot, but I am not one of them. This however is purely an opinion and there appears to be no golden rule on the subject.

Tip 12: The Accuracy Check:

I have emphasized the necessity of accuracy previously and now I'm going to do it again. The golden rule is that if you are writing 'Historical Fiction' then someone out there has either lived at the time of your setting, or has become an expert on this particular period in history, and written about it. Be assured, if there are some off-centre events embedded within your book that contradict the real events of the time, someone will tell you about it. The only get-out may be the fact that your theme encompasses some level of Science Fiction (a' la Dr Who) and a particularly useful time travel element. In fiction writing, I have found accuracy to be the key to quality and a provider of confidence to the reader. It takes a little research time, but the results far outweigh the effort spent and you will be much happier with your finished work in the long run. To my mind, accuracy is a key element to producing good fiction and in this modern communications age, there is little or no excuse not to be accurate!

Tip 13: The Main Character:

Fortunately there is no hard and fast rule relating to the creation of a character. The individual is part of the story, a fiction story, all of which is contained within your head. It's generally accepted that if you are producing a fast paced action thriller, written around a tight plot, then the main character may need to be presented to the reader in some detail. If, however you are writing a science fiction novel, set some time in the far and distant future, you may need to do a lot of work on creating your lead character … enough to make the whole scenario believable. Whatever your main character does, it must be believable to the reader; this is the key. So, what does your character look like? A good start would be to put together a picture of the person and something along the lines of the following.

A *believable* name for the character
A history for the character; school, career etc.
A physical description of the character; tall, thin, short, fat etc.
The habits, family and foibles of the character
The motivations that drive your character
How the character will impact on the storyline
Likes and dislikes, fads & fetishes of the character
Marital situation or marital history of the character

An important point relating to how your main character will fit the plot and create excitement or tension within the storyline is how you introduce him or her to the reader. It's a fairly good idea not to simply place characters on the stage of your book with a well written bio in their hand … it simply won't be good enough! Your main character has to be 'alive' and 'electric' with a personality that will grip the reader at the first introduction. This doesn't mean they have to be jumping about with a pistol in one hand and a sword in the other on page two, but simply showing something to the reader that is different, set's him or her apart and provides potential for what is to come next. Your main character is your most important character and you will be relying on him or her to carry the story forward. If you are able to create a vibrant lead character your readers can identify with … hero, anti-hero or villain … then you will have mastered the most difficult practice of all.

Tip 14: The Supporting Characters:

It's often easy to forget to introduce the supporting characters to your readers but just as important to 'fill' them out in the same way as your main characters. I have found it's a good idea to ensure you are careful in making the way you flesh out your supporting 'actors' so that such padding adds pace to the storyline and plot; not slow it down. Quick, short bursts of information laid on the reader are decidedly better than one long descriptive episode. Some writers go to the extremes of actually visiting places their characters may have been born in terms of their history as a fictitious character, taking photographs of houses he or she may have lived in. The process, I am told, of having photographs on a pin-board in front of you as you write seemingly makes the characters real to the writer. This may of course be true, but I feel this is obviously a 'bridge too far' for most. However, if it works for you, then go ahead. Remember that 'research is king' and if taking this approach gets your juices going, then go for it! As I have been fortunate enough to travel widely right from the 60's through to the late 90's, nearly all the places described in my books I have been to at some time or other. This serves two useful purposes: one being the assurance of great confidence in knowing my way around most storyline locations, and the other allowing me to work quickly without having to refer to the Internet and a stock image of the Monte Carlo Casino for example, when needing to describe the entrance.

Part 3:
The Plan

If you have an idea for a novel and are really serious about telling the story, you may now need to make an important decision about how much planning you are going to do? Some would say to you, simply skip the planning stage and just start writing. My warning would be that although this can produce a result of sorts, it can also be a dangerous path, full of pitfalls and many unnecessary roadblocks. On the other hand, you could make a detailed outline or sketch, along with a chapter-by-chapter list of plot points and character descriptions. This is of course the 'sensible route' but also one that can be littered with just as many problems for some of us. The most important element of your plan will be 'time!'

******

Tip 15: What Time Do You Have?

Making the time to write your book could be a matter of straightforward time management. To the rich man, poor man, entrepreneur, office PA, policeman, fireman, 'TIME' is the common enemy in all our lives; no matter who you are, who you may be a partner to or who you work for; we all have the same number of hours in a day. It's up to you to manage the way you use this precious time. My advice would always be to print out your notes or original synopsis and put them down where you can see them. Having a visual reminder of what you are committed to and possibly the inroads already made can make a big difference to your results. Self motivation is *key*. I have a ring binder file for each project I'm working on containing a full sketch, key research elements and the odd character bio, with the name of the project printed on the front cover in bold capitals. It sits on my desk and is not removed until the project is complete and published. Every time I walk into my office, that file tells me I have work to do!

Tip 16: What Time Can You Spare?

If you have a busy schedule … and who doesn't, then try writing in fifteen minute increments. Many professional writers find they can write for fifteen minutes without editing what's just been written.

Whether you work from home or have to turn up at the office each day, make sure you mark out and ring-fence some time for yourself that can be used for writing. You can write in your lunch break, on the train to work, staying over at the office for just fifteen minutes a day or getting up that little bit earlier and fitting in a quarter of an hour before breakfast.

When at home, turn off your television! If you think you really must see a particular program, record it and watch it later without the commercials. If time management is a real issue for you, then watching television, when you could be writing, has no part in your life.

As I now write full time, I put aside every morning from seven o'clock until I have a minimum of one thousand finished words on the page. By finished words I mean written and edited down from maybe two or three thousand words of script. I find this way keeps the storyline moving in my mind and requires no re-reading of the previous day's work before 'pressing the keys'. By writing in this way and making this commitment, I am able to 'pace' a project knowing within a week or so how long it will take and when it will be ready for publishing.

Making time to write is an obvious key element in your goal to write a fiction novel. Making excuses not to find the time is a key element that will drag you down a path leading to failure. If you cannot find the time to realize your ambition then you may need to consider putting of such a project until you do.

Tip 17: How Many Words?

Historically, most agents and publishers would look for around 100,000 (100K) words or more in a good length novel. Within the psycho of the publisher is firmly engrained the all important 'cost' of a printed book, especially the first edition which would normally be a hard cover version. He needs to get your book out there with the lowest production costs and the best selling price. Publishers are always playing this juggling act and that's one of the reasons they employ highly paid editors whose job it is to slash as many words as possible out of your novel, without losing the storyline or affecting the style of writing. If, of course, you are self publishing, then you can plan the length of your novel to suit you. In the twentieth century, it was generally common for a regular reader of books to buy a printed work in hard cover or paperback and read at home during the weekends, in the bath and on the train to the office. If it was a particularly appealing book, many would read it from cover to cover in one session ... and some still do! However, in this modern world where readers look to finish a novel much more quickly by reading it in small, regular slices on electronic media, a novel will now be regarded as a work of around 60K or more; a Novella at between 20K and 40K with a short story clocking in at something below 20K. These figures are not cast in stone but are simply an accepted average. You would therefore be well advised to make the length of your novel part of your plan; it will save you lots of time at the edit stage and stop you getting 'carried away' at the writing stage.

Remember, less is more and is it better to produce a fast paced 60K novel that readers will flock to purchase ... or a 150K epic work that possibly lacks pace, and will probably lack readers?

Tip 18: How Long To Complete?

This question is an important one and an answer lies in the combination of how many words you plan to write, what time you have available and what percentage of that time you can spare to write your manuscript. The calculation is a straightforward one. If you can write for two hours a day at a rate of 300 words an hour, you can produce around 3,000 words in ten hours, 30,000 words in 100 hours and a full length 60,000 word novel in around 200 hours.

If you can commit to five writing sessions of two hours each in a seven day week, then your book or novel is going to take 20 weeks to complete. If you have been doing a first edit as you go along, you can add another five weeks for the final edit and you will then have a finished manuscript in around 25 weeks ... or approximately five months. By making sure you have a timescale in your plan, it will give you a target to aim for. This therefore becomes part of a plan to succeed ... and not part of a plan to fail!

Tip 19: Producing A Sketch?

If you want an easy life; if you want to finish the work you so desperately started as a fiction novelist, try not to leave your writing process open to abuse. If you do, the person who will abuse it most will be you. You will blame the corresponding result on just about everyone else … of course, but the offender will actually be YOU! Do yourself a big favor and write a detailed sketch *'before'* you start on your five or six month writing journey.

Part 4:
The Sketch

The process of writing a sketch is straightforward. I have referred to it a few times up to this point because a sketch is something that will assist you to write effectively, provide support for your writing process and most importantly … keep you sitting in front of that laptop producing *good* work. You may find you have the sort of confidence that will allow you to do without this excellent tool in your toolbox, and if you can that is fantastic. However, if you are in any doubt at all about your ability to sit straight down and write a 60,000 word manuscript, without anything other than a great idea in your head, please think again.

******

Tip 20: What Is A Sketch?

A sketch is a document that many may call a 'synopsis' or 'story line'. However, a sketch from my viewpoint is much more than a synopsis, or a collection of carefully crafted story notes. It has the depth and roundness of a complete short story with references where required to character function, plot development, the beginning, middle and end definition of the story and very importantly, relevant references to your research file. Everything you will need to complete your sketch will be found in your set of 'Subject' folders. As previously described, your folders will contain information that is researched or collated to create the foundation of your writing project. As a quick reminder, the minimum number of folders could be entitled as follows: *Manuscript, Research, Sketch, Images, Maps, Downloads and Character Profiles.*

Tip 21: Producing A Sketch:

The folders titled 'Manuscript' and 'Sketch' are self explanatory. The 'Research' folder will contain all your research notes from say 'the Internet' or information and data 'CD's. This can encompass subject matter relating to the setting for the story, the education and background of your characters, how poisons work and even how a specific firearm operates.

The 'Images' folder will probably contain images relating to the scenario such as pictures of a particular town at a certain time in history. Other images may be of how people in a specific country dressed around a set of dates and maybe even some satellite images of an actual country, including road networks and street names etc.

The 'Maps' folder will probably store maps and

geography of countries involved in your story, possibly confirming travel routes between countries. They will enable you to calculate distances and time in relation to your character as he or she moves through various countries or parts of a specific country. Having your main character travel by train, from New York to say Chicago in a couple of hours, will not go down well with a fussy reader.

Having a 'Downloads' folder to keep a track of internet downloads is always a good idea. It gives you a hot link back to the source of your research in case you need more information from the same website.

A place to keep all your character profiles is essential. Maintain a folder entitled 'Character Profiles' and keep it updated as you write with new or different attributes you discover about them or allocate to them.

Tip 22: Essential Elements:

The essential elements of a good sketch are a story line that is blessed with a beginning, a middle and an end. The 'Sketch' will need to 'set the scene' for your story; introduce the characters involved in the narrative and 'set the pace' at which the manuscript will develop. This is why a sketch is valuable because in the writing of it, you can 'test' every element of the story to see if it actually works. Just to keep on top of it, label the three necessary parts of it as the beginning, middle and end. Don't forget, there are also three important things you would be wise to outline within these three parts of your sketch, and they are back-story, characters, and plot.

Sticking to these basics will provide you with a 'tight' sketch and a great platform from which you can begin writing your manuscript. A good sketch will iron out many of the anomalies that may exist in your mind about how certain characters interact with one another and how their activities affect the unraveling of the main plot.

Tip 23: Capacity To Surprise:

The words 'hook' and 'reveal' used often by reviewers when commenting on the elements of a novel such as a thriller or murder mystery, can often be boiled down to the basic ability of the author to write with a capacity to surprise. If you are not able to provide the right amount of 'surprise' in the thirty or so pages of a sketch, you will definitely not achieve that much sought after attribute in say four hundred pages of your final manuscript.

The way to ensure your sketch contains situations and scenarios that lead to a 'surprise' of some description, or necessary but unexpected twist in the general plot is to put it down after ten pages and don't pick it up again for three or four days. Then, pick it up and read as if it is actually a short story you've not read before. If 'surprise' is present, you will recognize it. If it's not, the likely hood is you will find the place where it should be. Because you know your story so well ... in your head ... it's sometimes difficult to identify the 'surprise element' in the thousands of words that have been rattling round your consciousness for possibly months. When in doubt, my recommendation would always be to 'put it down' and pick it up later with a clear head and a more objective viewpoint.

The capacity to surprise is a major target to aim for in your manuscript. It means the difference between producing a good book and a great book. Don't forget that often 'surprise' is not necessarily about the content of your plot or storyline but more about the way you reveal the various elements of your story to the reader. It's an important point and it's good to make sure you have it contained within your sketch.

Tip 24: Being The Reader:

It's always worth remembering the writer's golden thought ... *The reader does not know what is coming next!* So it's the capacity to surprise and the twists and turns of the plot that will keep him or her reading that extra page or two when a lesser offering will have been put down ... and possibly not picked up again. Put yourself in the position of the reader ...

your customer ... when evaluating your sketch. If it still excites you, there is every reason to assume it will excite your reader. Be creative, be adaptive and be your own worst critic. Producing a good sketch will enable you ... the writer ... to see the 'wood' through the 'trees' and the trees only get thicker the more pages of your manuscript you get down on the screen. Your reader likes clear, concise writing, thrilling action and a plot that holds their interest to the very last page. Ironing out any possible lapses into boredom at the sketch stage will be invaluable in producing a working manuscript your readership will welcome.

Tip 25: Editing A Sketch:

This should be a 'no-brainer'. Its common sense to take a view that editing a ten or twelve thousand word sketch is a much more amenable task than a 'deep cut' edit on a full blown 60K to 70K manuscript. As highlighted above, simply seeing the wood through the trees is half the battle ... and not getting so fed up with making thousands of corrections on your lengthy manuscript ... before throwing it in the bin ... is another! Take your sketch seriously and edit down the well directed skeleton story line and plot that will be fleshed out to become your finished novel. One word of advice; don't bother with grammar ... just get the words right, the story flowing and the smile on your face. Grammar is a technicality that can be corrected in the final edit ... excitement is something unique and cannot be injected into your sketch by a piece of software.

Tip 26: Finalizing A Sketch:

When you come to the point where you have written your sketch and edited it, you may need to check the following:

Is your story sketch divided in to specific sections?
Do your characters have credibility?
Is the setting properly researched?
Do you have a beginning, middle and end?
Have you decided on a target manuscript length?
Most importantly ... do you like it?

So assuming you are happy with your sketch, the next move is to simply put it away and don't think about it again for about two weeks. Then ...pick it up ... and read it again. If you still like it ... start writing it! If for any reason the bells of warning start ringing, and doubt begins to set in ... start again!

Tip 27: Without A Sketch:

If you are one of those rare but fortunate individuals who do not require any level of preparation before getting down to the hard work of tackling your new manuscript, then you will possibly not have bothered with producing a sketch. If that is the case, or if you simply don't like the discipline and time involved in producing a detailed preliminary of your intended work, then I urge you not to ignore the basic rules of preparation ... which are ... *Be organized, Know your subject* and *Manage your time.*

Part 5:
Before You Start

The process of writing a sketch will have given you a taste for the characters and the storyline. You may love them, but will others think the same? So, before you start into your manuscript, why not have some people read your sketch? They will hopefully give you an unbiased opinion, make suggestions and perhaps provide feedback about your writing style. Whatever you actually do, there are several areas to consider before you commit to a full manuscript. Paying attention to these important areas will save you much time and possibly anguish later … you can bet on it!

******

Tip 28: Can You Actually Write?

This may seem to be a rather pointless question but it is a genuine one. Most individuals can put pen to paper, write a coherent letter to their bank manager and even knock out the odd essay or short story or two, perhaps even good enough to be found gracing the pages of your local newspaper. However, the ability to put tens of thousands of words together in a fashion that will make the reader want to keep turning to the next page is another can of worms completely. There's help out there on the Internet for writers, of all levels of talent, to assist with editing, grammar, formatting and structure. If you have any misgivings whatsoever, try and connect with someone who writes for a living and is willing to assist you before you start your manuscript. You will then gain the benefit of some professional input from the very beginning. Writing is a lonely business and not many around you … who demand some of your time on a regular basis … will be able to understand why you want to do it. If you can find a mentor or join an active writing group, this is an excellent way to get started and guarantee you will actually finish. None of us are perfect … we all need help! If you seek it out, you may be surprised to find how much support there is out there.

Tip 29: Your Writing Format:

I have always felt it's important to decide on the format of your manuscript before getting down to it. 'Why?' You may well ask. The reason is that as your manuscript takes shape, if formatted correctly in Word, for example, you will begin to see how it will look to the reader. If you are writing for print and EBook, then you may wish to format your manuscript for print and then convert for EBook. This is how I do it, finding it's the best way round as the process is easier and provides less room for error. One initial decision point will be to determine the size of the print paperback. A general industry standard is 6 inches x 9 inches but I have found that one generally good size for most paperback novels up to around 350/400 pages is 5 inches x 8 inches. So, if formatting your manuscript for print, set the page size, set the gutter and mirror margins and complete the header with a title and author and footer with a page number. Set the font to something sensible like Times Roman at 12pt and single line space or 12.5 pt and a 1.15 line space. It would be a good idea to set the paragraph with a 3 to 4 point indent and not to use repeat returns for a new paragraph. If you do, the indents can become uneven and may cause a problem with reformatting for EBook later.

Tip 30: Writing To Sell?

To the writer and novelist of course, every word they write is blindingly commercial and readers will be flooding Amazon with so many orders when their new work is released, the website itself will crash in overload. Unfortunately, I can guarantee that this will not be the case. The most popular self published EBook categories at the time of writing still remain thriller, mystery and then romance. But the publishing business is very fickle and best selling genres can change overnight. The secret is of course to know what the next best selling genre will be … and then write a novel for it. Producing a character that has 'legs' and can be the central figure in a series of novels in episodic format is also a popular way to go. If you are writing to sell in substantial numbers ... then you will need to research what is selling now ... and what is forecast to sell in 12 months time. Producing a best-selling novel is not purely a matter of talent ... it's much more a matter of luck. The more you research what you should be writing, the luckier you will get.

Tip 31: Writing For Vanity?

Maybe you have no ambition for your work other than to see it published and have some printed copies, with a nice glossy cover, to hand round at parties and send to all your friends at Christmas. If this is the case, then you have the freedom to write as you wish, write as you feel you should, and write simply as you consider guided. But beware ... and do not fall into the trap of self satisfaction that will possibly hide or at the very least mask your writing abilities to such an extent that others close to you may not recognize the writer at all. If the process of writing for vanity is to hold any merit, it must surely be that a piece of you has been put to paper for all time ...not some unrecognizable individual who writes only for self titillation. This often applies to vanity works in the Romance, Historical Fiction and Erotica genres.

Tip 32: Writing A Epic?

It's tempting of course …! The 250,000 word blockbuster will represent maybe years of work to get to a publishing point, but beware, as this effort may only see you receiving 70% of a title price of $9.99 and unless you are lucky enough to sell an awful lot of covers, you will not see a sensible reward for all that hard work from your EBook sales. The calculation is easy to understand. If you are going to make money from selling EBooks on line, at prices from $2.99 to $4.99, then you need to produce more of them than if you were fortunate enough to have a hard copy traditional publishing deal where every man and his close associate within the publishing company is working their socks off to sell your masterpiece for you.

You may only end up with say 30% of the title price on a standard publishing deal, but that price could be well over $29.99 initially … and then there are the translation sales in twenty or so countries to consider. So, the simple answer … without a traditional publishing deal … is to produce more work. For the E-novelist the way to go is to produce shorter novels and publish them more frequently. The market is currently looking for shorter novels as reading habits change and attention spans wither. For the time and energy taken up in producing one superbly flowing 100,000+ word epic, published once a year at $9.99 a time, you could produce several 30K to 50K word novels at $3.99. The choice is yours, but if you really want to make a living as an EBook Writer and Paperback Novelist, then my advice would be to get the work out there on a regular basis.

Tip 33: Quality Expectations:

Quality over quantity? Is what I have just said about to be contradicted? No. The best sellers of just about everything put a high value on quality. So even if you are now producing five or six books ... but shorter books ... a year, they still need to be of sustainable quality. Who decides what 'Quality' really is? Well ..., to my way of thinking, you do. If you are happy with your work, it can be guaranteed that an editor will not be. But he or she will have a different agenda to you ... especially if they are working on behalf of the publisher! Do not be persuaded by any third party that quality is lacking if you have done a job and done it well. In reality, *you* know what is good enough and what is not. Be hard on yourself in the edit, check the final output carefully and be proud to have your name attached to it. That's the very best quality assurance guarantee you can wish for.

Tip 34: Do You Want To Sell It?

Well, as Shakespeare might have put it "There lies the rub!" because if you want to sell your work as a self-published author, you may need a little help. Fortunately, we have the Internet and Social Media to assist along the way ... and these services are all generally FREE.! If you want to become purely an EBook author for example, you will have to work hard in between your 'authoring' phases. You will probably need a website or at least a blog to direct your readers to. You will also need a Twitter, Face Book or other prominent social media account to tell the world you are part of it. Maintaining these promotional platforms can be time consuming, but it's a lot cheaper than employing a PR agency, or paying for lot's of click-through fees ... and a lot more cost effective. But don't forget the real plus ... It's all mostly FREE.

Selling your newly produced book really is the hard part, but the general message will be to get your work out on as many platforms as possible. Don't stop at Amazon when there is Barnes & Noble out there for example. Seek out the numerous on-line EBook platforms on the Internet and choose wisely, but choose you must to get the coverage you need to launch your work. There is much more on this subject contained within the hundreds of advice websites out there on the Internet particularly directed to authors. You will also find this subject approached again later in more detail.

Tip 35: The Time Plan:

In sections 15 and 16 we talk about time and its importance to the writer. You will need a 'time plan' before you start and this is the one key element that will allow you to start … and finish your sketch and the follow-on manuscript. When considering what to do 'before you start', make sure you have a 'Time Plan' … and one that will actually work. It's no use setting yourself a time plan of twenty hours a week when you know from the outset that this is totally impossible. Consult with your partner, talk to the children; make everyone part of your project so they will be there supporting you and not wondering why you suddenly seem to have deserted them. If this is not your first offering, you will already have been there …so this message could perhaps be considered as 'preaching to the converted!'

I have talked about time planning before and I will no doubt mention it again before the end of this book of '101 Fiction Writing Tips'. Making time to write is such an important issue with most well intended writers that its worthwhile remembering many full time professional writers and authors encounter the same time management problems as you!

Tip 36: The Organization Plan:

In sections 1 and 2 we talk about being 'Organized'

You will need to have your plan in place, your folders easily searchable and your storyline in clear mental relief ... 'before you start'. If you are organized, you will find yourself at the end of your detailed sketch before you know it. If you are not, then you may simply give in to all those annoying, but constant voices around you eager to confirm you are wasting your time. Don't give in ... be organized! Let me assure you that all your family, friends and work colleagues genuinely and sincerely want you to be a successful author. However, they don't want you to do on their time! Be strong, be determined ... be organized!

Tip 37: Finalize The Working Title:

Why ... you may ask, is it necessary to finalize a title for your new epic novel when you are only writing the first sketch? Well, from my point of view, it locks you in to the story, it forces you to think about how the whole project will need to be managed and most importantly, it allows you to research possible competition for the title and even discover if there may even be a storyline out there so similar to your own, that some would consider uncanny ... and others consider plagiarism. You really want a title that has little or no competition within Internet search engines so that when you are up there on Amazon, your title arrives first in any search for the specific words or anything similar. Having the title researched and confirmed, before you start, can be a bonus in terms of satisfaction, knowing you are working on something real, something which has substance and the self generating energy to carry you through to the very end.

Tip 38: Title Conflict:

Whatever you may think initially, as a self-published writer, I am quite sure you will gain a real advantage in the comfort of knowing there is no other title out there that conflicts in any way with yours. This is the real aim. Simply put the proposed title into a search engine and check the result. If there are lots of titles or word combinations coming up, related in some way to yours, you may experience a poor search result for your newly published book with older, similar and more established titles gaining those important first few listings. This is not a good position to be in and can often be salvaged by thinking hard about the title for your proposed novel and making the relevant changes. For example, if you put the word 'murder' into Amazon.com search, you will receive around 90,000 results. If you add the word 'files' to make 'murder files', then you will have dramatically reduced the result to around 2,700. If you add the word 'Williams' to make the search phrase 'Williams murder files' … (which could be the title of your book) … then the result is down to single figures. The very best situation to be in is not to have one single title in the whole publishing world the same as yours. This aspiration is however not so easy to rise to, so my recommendation would be to give this subject some of your valuable time … it's well worth it!

Part 6:
The Manuscript

Now you have completed your sketch, you will no doubt be eager to start work on your manuscript. This is, in effect, a straightforward process that with a standard knowledge of Word, or the word processing program you are using in your writing project, will be fairly easy to set up. However, there could be one or two things to consider before you get 'stuck in' to the very first chapter … and some of them are listed here.

******

Tip 39: Print Or EBook?

The answer to this question will dictate how you should best format your manuscript and set all the relevant defaults. As I have said before, there is no golden rule but it makes sense to set up your page for print and then convert the final manuscript for EBook. It's easier to do and will not normally affect primary settings such as indents and line spacing etc. If you are not writing for print, then you will normally be free to work in standard Letter or A4 page size with normal margins. If writing for a print production, it can often be easier to download a template from the Internet if you're unsure of things like Gutters, Mirror margins and Page Breaks etc.

One tip in relation to templates is that when you first look at the template in your WP program, it will be a good idea to view it with paragraph marks and other hidden symbols set to 'show'. In 'Word', the tab is shown as a Paragraph mark in the 'Paragraph' tabs box. By doing this you will not only see the marks but the section breaks and page breaks that you will need to manage as the manuscript progresses.

Tip 40: Agent Or Self-Publish?

If you are fortunate enough to have the services of an experienced agent, he or she will no doubt provide you with a set of criteria in relation to setting up your manuscript. If you are self-publishing, then make sure you read the help and advice section of the publishing facilitator such as Amazon, KDP etc. They have some great, easy to understand advice sections and FAQ's on setting up your manuscript so that when you submit it to them there will be minimal chance of rejection. Follow the relevant instructions carefully as they are designed to limit the amount of hassle you may experience as you load up your .doc or .pdf files to the web. Some conversion programs, for example, may not accept any tab marks at the beginning of new paragraphs. Others may limit the maximum font size for the title and chapter headings. There can also be a limit on the attributes of a .pdf file conversion and you may have to reset them on your PC before making a direct conversion from Word or another WP program. Some current on-line convertors will only accept .doc and .docx or later Word files and so if you are using another type of software, you may need to be careful with compatibility. You will need to be particularly diligent with uploading to "Smashwords" but there is an excellent downloadable file available to tell you exactly how to format your manuscript for submission to their site.

Tip 41: Default Setting For Print:

One of the problem areas for most facilitators offering a POD (Print On Demand) service is that not all provide an automatic edit facility. So it's a very good idea to make sure you have set your complete document to the default settings required by the provider of the service ... and not just 'the section'..! It's easy to do as you stroll through to the end of your work to find that when you view the uploaded manuscript on the site viewer, the layout is all over the place and indents either disappeared or half a sentence long! This is a common issue and some good advice would be that when you have conquered this problem, save the document as a template. This will keep the page and document settings ready for your next project.

Tip 42: Choose A Font:

Choosing a font for your manuscript is a fairly straightforward affair. It goes without saying that using a flowery or block font such as Chanson or Accent, will not be acceptable. Twelve point, Times New Roman proportional font is very popular or, Courier New, mono-spaced font if your agent or publisher specifies a font that occupies the same amount of space vertically and horizontally. Make sure your font is black … no colors. You will find the settings box for your fonts on the 'Home' page of Word and this is where you will find it on most other WP software. Avoid fancy script fonts and lots of changes in size formatting. Remember the reader? Yes, they have to read it … so make it a comfortable experience on the eye.

Tip 43: Set Margins To Suit Output:

A one-inch margin on all four sides with a paper size setting of A4 or Letter is the default in most WP programs. If you asked a publisher or maybe an agent, "what is a standard paperback trim size?" they would probably tell you "6 inches x 9 inches", although as I have said previously, I personally prefer 5 x 8. However, today's modern standard is to work in metric formats, which makes the 6×9 inches pattern convert to approx 15.2cm x 22.8cm. The script area for a standard 12 point font of say Times New Roman on a 6x9 setting will be approx 10.5cm x 17.5cm. You therefore will need to set your margins all round to approx 2.5cm to obtain this page layup on an A4/Letter page size. If you are going to have your book printed, then the 'gutter' margin, which is the side against which the finished work will be bound, will need to be greater in width for obvious reasons. Best advice would be to consult your publisher directly or check the page setup requirements of the Self Publishing website. As stated in Tip 39, if you are going straight to EBook and have no intention of moving to print, then you can make margins to suit your own requirements.

Tip 44: Set Indents:

Default indentations are half an inch or approx 1.25cm. This tab is preset in most word processing software programs and as such is normally required by publishers. However, if for some reason you need to change this setting, you can generally do so on the 'Home' page on the top line of the paragraph tab box. I normally like to use smaller indents and go for three points rather than a size. The preference is obviously yours as long as you ensure there are no tab marks on the opening of a new paragraph.

Tip 45: Set Line Spacing:

It's obvious you can write in any space set up you like. Many writers set up for double spacing when producing a manuscript, but some write in single or

1.15 space to have an idea as the work progresses, how long, in terms of number of pages, the final project will be. If when using Times Roman you find the bottom of the 'g' being cut off as it reads on the page, then you will need to increase line spacing a little. Remember, no matter how you choose to write, submissions to an agent or publisher would normally be double spaced with no extra line spaces between paragraphs. However, as part of the revolution in publishing and gradual advance of publishers into the 21st Century, this requirement is now often waved.

Tip 46: Alignment:

Many writers will tell you the manuscript page should be set to Align left and *not* justified. The right edges will *not* be uniform or even, but that's OK. However, there is a preference from many who self publish to write the manuscript for print with justified margins, so the choice fall back is simply what you are really most comfortable with. Whatever you decide, the final manuscript provided for submission to EBook will need to be justified. Be careful here if you have been using a left alignment as converting to justified may mess up some word spacing. It's a good idea to check the whole document, with all hidden marks displayed, after this change.

Tip 47: Page Headers:

In the page 'Header' you can place a title of the work and the copyright symbol for example, next to the year and name of the author for submission to an agent or publisher only. If you are self publishing, you can alternate each header with your name on one and the book title on the other in a manuscript destined for print. If you are only looking to publish an electronic file for Kindle or similar, then you will need to consider an EBook is a seamless and continuous read and therefore will not require 'headers' or page numbers inserted into the footer.

Tip 48: Page Footers:

It's common to place page numbers after the title page. However, there are no hard and fast rules on the subject. Whatever WP software you are using, you can normally find the page numbering tab on the 'Insert' page in the Header & Footer block. If you don't know how to start page numbering from a page other than the very first one, you will need to ensure that your manuscript contains sections and the first pages with the title and acknowledgments etc are placed in the first 'section'. You then create a new 'section' on the page your work starts and the numbering begins. If unsure, please enter a query by hitting the help icon; there are plenty of good bits of advice there. If you are only writing for EBook, then you will not suffer from this issue as there will be no page numbers in your final manuscript.

Tip 49: Scene Breaks:

Don't forget scene breaks in your manuscript and a good way to indicate them is by inserting a blank line and centering say six 'Star' signs normally found above the number eight on an English computer keyboard. My advice at this point would be to try and avoid inserting fancy scene and chapter breaks that are in effect 'images'. This may cause your manuscript to be rejected when being converted by your chosen on-line publishing software. If you are inserting an 'image' into your written manuscript, there may well be certain quality requirements generated by the conversion software. If your electronic submission fails because of this, you will normally be shown a message. The easiest way to *not* encounter this issue is *not* to use images as scene breaks. Keeping your final presentation simple and un-elaborate, especially in EBook format is an essential part of making the reader experience a 'comfortable' one. A comfortable reader is usually a happy reader and that's the type you are looking for! Distractions are not required … and fancy scene break and chapter heading images can be a distraction for some people.

Tip 50: New Chapters:

If your manuscript is set up for print, then it will require you to begin chapters on new pages by inserting a page break. A standard format normally requires you to center the chapter title, even if it's only Chapter One (or Chapter 1), at the top of the page in say a size 24/28 point. Skip a couple of spaces and begin the text of the chapter. Centering is not a golden rule and you can obviously place a chapter heading wherever you wish. However, you may need to note that some processes for print restrict the maximum size of font that can be used in a submitted manuscript. This is also the case in the production of some EBook formats, so check it out before you start. A word of warning; if you do not use page breaks and simply tab down from the last line to a new page, you may have problems formatting back from print to EBook. Again, with chapter headings it's a good idea to avoid fancy fonts and imported 'bars' as underlines. The bars are generally stored as images within your WP program, and in avoiding them you avoid conversion problems.

Tip 51: Words With Emphasis:

It's often a difficulty choosing how to 'emphasize' words in your manuscript. Many writers use italics for emphasized words unless an agent or publisher requests underlining, and it's now common to only use a single space rather than two spaces after periods. The habit of some to emphasize words by making them 'Bold' is not a good one. Using 'CAPITALS' is also not recommended and such small points, if not managed properly can get your manuscript rejected by an agent or publisher if it's a first submission. How you emphasize or give strength to your words or even complete sentences is up to you, but whatever method you decide upon, make sure it's consistent throughout the manuscript.

Tip 52: Multiple Periods:

This is a difficult one. The use of more than one period to emphasize part of a line of script, the trailing off in a line of conversation or indicating a pause in an exchange or thought, is becoming more common. Depending on your software, a series of more than three periods may be highlighted as a grammatical error. There is only one rule which is … if you are happy with it then that's the only requirement. So … if you use periods, like I have done here … and you are happy that such an event indicator will be accepted by your readers, then make the very best use of it. I personally use it a lot and many individuals describe its use as 'lazy grammar'. However, as I read … I write and therefore find it serves the right purpose.

Tip 53: The End:

What happens when your manuscript actually comes to an end? What you should do is simply write '*The End*' as you want agents and editors to know they've reached the end of your manuscript and there are no more chapters or epilogues to come. For EBook only manuscripts, it's simply a common courtesy to let the reader know that you have finished telling him ... or her, your story.

Part 7:
The Writers' Diseases

There are of course many writers' diseases you should endeavor to inoculate yourself against. The result of catching one may simply cost you an irritating but short loss of time which means your manuscript will take longer to produce than originally planned. In the very worst case, the writer will give up altogether. There is one thing to remember in relation to anything that invades or attacks your plan, and in any way stops you writing. No matter who you blame, in the final count, it will only be *you* inflicting this curse upon yourself.

******

Tip 54: Self Doubt:

If you are unfortunate enough to catch the common winter virus of self doubt, unless you find a way of attacking it immediately, then your writing plan will go 'out of the window', your time plan will dissolve into nothingness and eventually, you will stop writing completely. So, if you don't actually believe in yourself anymore, should anyone really care? If you doubt you have the ability to write … having gone through all the pain and time consuming research to put your writing project together, then things will not get better on their own. Self doubt is generated by a lack of confidence in your ability to put words on a page in a reasonable order to the extent they make sense to the reader. Self doubt can also be spawned by others around you constantly providing you with advice you really don't need. There's more later!

Tip 55: Writers' Block:

Writers' block is now recognized as the second stage of self doubt. If you do nothing about the 'self doubt' virus, you will definitely move on to the 'writer's block' stage. There is more on writers block later but in effect if you doubt your preparation, if you doubt the sincerity of your ability to put words down on a page, if you doubt you will ever have the time to finish your manuscript ... then the result will be failure.

Tip 56: Ditching The Plan:

The point of desperation you will no doubt face on not being able to 'un-block' yourself will be to ditch the plan. You will blame 'the plan' for all of your woes and the evil voice inside your head will be pushing you to take another path ... in other words ... 'ditch the plan!' Once you do that, you are a rudderless ship in a stormy ocean. Unfortunately, as you alone act as captain and crew, you have no-one to hand your responsibilities to ...so then, when you have reached this desperate point, you simply have to resort to the dreaded excuse of 'not enough time!'

Tip 57: Not Enough Time:

So here you are. All your planning and exhaustive sketching has now ended up in the toilet because you 'simply don't have the time'. The excuse is a winner of course with family, friends, children, mothers, brothers, sisters, husbands and wives who have all been robbed of your precious time whilst you have been 'head down – backside in the air' constructing the necessary planning disciplines and framework for your writing project. The winter virus has turned into a major disease ... and one for which there is no cure. Not one single person will be around you who can catch it, leaving you with no one you can discuss the situation with and therefore ... life goes on. The only person disappointed with you ... *is now you.!*

Part 8:
Self Doubt

The start of it all is of course when you have lost the convincing ambition that first drove you to put pen to paper in the first place. Self doubt comes from becoming lost in the process, not being organized and generally being harassed by those around you who are not fully 'on board' with your particular writing ambition. Read on!

******

Tip 58: Lost Belief:

There are many writers, or would be writers out there who are so taken up with their own abilities and therefore fantastic potential, they regularly fail to live up to such expectations. So, in effect, you end up being disappointed with yourself when you see the words staring back at you from the printed page. At this point you should not 'Give Up' ... you should 'Buck Up'... but how should you 'Buck Up?'

Firstly, it's worth remembering no one has time to listen to your problems and those around you will have no inkling you have caught the self doubt virus. Some good advice would be *not* to go round moaning and groaning to everyone you meet ... *they are simply not interested* in the fact that you will shoot to the top of the best sellers list '*if*' you could only solve this one small plot or character issue.

You may need to take on board that you are probably not the centre of anyone's universe ... except your own. Unless you are famous and your name trips easily from everyone's lips in general conversation, then ... to be frank with you, from my experience, no one really gives a damn!

You may of course consider yourself ... with the growing thrust of ambition, to be the best writer in the world but no one else will think so until you are made rich and famous due to the 'loads of money' earned through your published work. When you reach that point, rest assured, you will be the centre of attention for millions ... in company with the Tax man.

Review your previous work constructively. Tell yourself the truth! Is it good ... or not? If you are serious about writing, you will know. The act of ripping out text is therapeutic, simply because you know the end result will be a positive one.

When you are plagued with self doubt, it's a good idea, when in the company of others, to not make yourself a pain in the backside by constantly going on about your 'new novel' and your 'next new book'. No one wants to know. Take note of the wise words above. Instead of talking endlessly about yourself and your writing when in company, take time out to 'listen' to others around you putting you in the comfortable position of having your next great character created for you and gathering much needed material for your next epic novel. I can tell you from experience that being asked 'what you do?' ... and replying 'I'm a writer!' ... does not float many boats. In fact when you tell them that's what you do, they mostly carry on a conversation, ignoring you, or issue the obligatory ... 'That's nice' ... and then move quietly away. Being a writer is a lonely, highly disciplined business and your best friend and most honest critic has to be you!

Tip 59: Giving Up:

The easy route? Well, not really. Even the process of 'giving up' will have its consequences. If you lean toward a tendency to give up when things get a bit tough, then you will never become a recognised fiction author. Simply giving up is not in the DNA of the established writer, and if you wish to get to such a position, then there is no room for negative attitude.

Tip 60: No Mentor:

With or without the mental strength to plough through obstacles to reach your final goal, there is no doubt whatsoever, if you have a mentor to turn to, especially in difficult times, you will stand a much better chance of succeeding ... and actually finishing your manuscript. If you do not have someone you know who is already an established writer, search the social media and see if you can find a person in your local area already producing work on a regular basis. Another way of course is to put out a request on FaceBook or Twitter for a mentor. Other writers may be happy to mentor you ... or they may not, but from my best knowledge, I have found that many will be happy to pass on their experiences and review your work ... as long as you do not become a *pest*! Don't forget your local writing circle or club. Whatever you do, make contact with them ... you may find just what you're looking for.

Part 9:
Writers' Block

I touched on this earlier and I'm afraid the bad news is that 'writers block' can kill your project more or less immediately. You then risk falling into the category of one of those failed writers in your late teens or early twenties who give up their dream and go back to it some 30 or 40 years later. But at this stage, you may be blessed with children now grown and the advantage that general family will then be too involved with their own lives to bother much about the shaded corners of yours. You will no doubt also keep the revival of your writing project a secret … it's just the way it is … and it happens much more often that you would think. The good news is, when 'writers block' hits you at this stage … there is a way through it!

Tip 61: Stop Writing:

The 'stop writing' technique is exactly what it says on the tin … simply *stop* writing and do something else. Yes, you read correctly. Stop writing, spend time with the family and simply relax. Just about every writer will have experienced WB at least once in their writing career, and most will tell you their way of overcoming the problem is simply to stop work completely and leave the whole project alone for maybe a week, or even longer.

'But when do you know when to go back to it?' You may ask. Well the answer is, you will know when after a few days, you may be sitting quietly on the sofa, with a large gin and tonic in hand … and suddenly it will come to you. Whatever was a block, restricting the pursuance your story line, will probably flash in front of you … you will see the words clearly, and you will rush to find a pen and paper to ensure they are captured and protected from an unsure and unreliable memory. Problem solved! This is the 'common cure' and is similar to a battery re-charge because sometimes you can become too involved with your project and stepping back from it for a short while allows your mind to move to refresh mode releasing a clear, unrestricted view through the trees to the 'wood' beyond. It works in nine cases out of ten.

Tip 62: Jolt Therapy:

Give your mind a jolt by writing over and over again … 'I need to expand on my idea like this …' If there is something there … it will come … quickly. You may be smiling at this one but if you know any writers, ask them if they have used this technique at any time in the past … and a sensible bet will be the answer 'Yes'. It's a bit like writing out lines at school; you eventually become so angry with yourself that something new suddenly appears on the page. Problem solved!

Tip 63: Something Different:

Write something different. If you are in the middle of a heavy novel, stop and write a few limericks. If you are on page three of a self-help extravaganza, stop and write an amusing letter to a friend. Simply changing your train of thought will bring about a release to allow a whole new set off words to appear tumbling out of your darker mental recesses and spreading out on the page before you. This is a very common solution to writers block and is generally effective. I use this technique in a slightly different way by working on two books in parallel. When I feel a bit stuck on one ... I simply move over and work on the other. This resolves well for me because as I write on a regular basis, I can make the time to spend on moving from one manuscript to another.

Tip 64: Talk About It:

The obvious, but often misunderstood process of talking through your problem gels with the need to have a mentor or be part of a writing club or circle. If such an advantage eludes you, make attempts to get hold of someone who is interested in you and your writing. Put the problem of your block to them ... and see if they can come up with a way out. Remember, two heads are often better than one. Having someone to talk with about your passion is invaluable and I am fortunate to know several professional writers who generously allow me to 'unload' on them now and again, as well as bouncing a few ideas around the park from time to time.

Tip 65: The Answer Is In The Sketch:

No, the sketch has not been forgotten and the really good thing about writing one is that when problems loom on the horizon, you will have a comprehensive and finished piece of work to refer to. When searching for inspiration, look to your sketch first. The answer will often be resting there, sometimes hidden … and sometimes leaping out of the page. The best and most useful way to tackle your search is not to skim though the whole document, looking for the elusive phrase or sentence, but to read it, page by page from beginning to end. This will do two things. Firstly, it will refresh your mind in relation to what the whole story is all about … character by character. Secondly, reading the sketch again will force you to evaluate what you have already written in your manuscript. Perhaps what you are looking for is simply 'not there' because it was never meant to be. Reading the sketch will inevitably force your thoughts back on to the straight and narrow and hopefully finally put to bed the disease of 'writers block' for the rest of your story telling journey.

Part 10:
Is It Good Enough?

Now you have 'unblocked' yourself, you will have a need to get on and finish your writing project. What one single word describes the qualities you now need to close off that final page, place that final full stop and open that last bottle of chilled Chardonnay? That word is 'Dedication!' This is what drives you, feeds you and will finally allow you to finish your book. Dedication feeds on 'passion' and the more you have of one the more you will be able to bring to the other. The dedication required to force yourself to 'hit the keyboard' every single day for months on end, to manage your own time ... whilst possibly being asked to constantly manage the time of others inside a busy family, brings its problems. Sometimes, such problems may seem insurmountable ... but dedication will allow you to achieve and therefore succeed. Your passion to be a recognised fiction author will be your comfort in such situations. If you have no passion, then dedication will be unable to 'take root'. Does this all sound a 'bit over the top' to you? Well I can assure you it's not as trite or clichéd as it initially appears ... and now you will need to be your own best critic by considering the following.

******

Tip 66: Is It Clear?

Being clear means that although you have a need to get down on paper what you want to say, it's always best to bear in mind, the person who is reading your published work does not know *what is coming next*. You must be clear in letting your reader know exactly what is happening in the storyline. Flowery and long descriptive paragraphs can confuse a reader and he or she does not particularly want to have to unravel a puzzle of words in order to find out what is going on with the plot or how a character is handling a specific situation. The simple, honest advice is to be 'Clear' about your subject matter, paragraph by paragraph and chapter by chapter. Pace and action in an historical novel, love story or spy thriller is moved on by the clarity of your writing. If you don't need the words … as you will find out next … take them out!

Tip 67: Is It Word Thrifty?

No matter how many times it's said, the first rule of good writing in general and fiction writing in particular, is to be thrifty with words. Make every single one count and simply put, be brief. Editing is the key and choosing a writing method where you edit as you go along, session by session, is often a good route to go, especially if you are new to the fiction writing experience. As you edit, search every sentence for a possibly different way of getting your message across. If your main character engages in long periods of conversation, it's a good idea to make sure that such conversation is lean and moves the story and plot forward. Try to side-step the trap of simply producing a series of words that 'bog down' the reader to the point where he or she loses all hope and put's your book down ... to not pick it up again! Finally, avoid like the plague producing a series of words simply to impress yourself, in the hope you may also impress others, as a demonstration of an excellent command of the English language.

Tip 68: Does It Have Style?

You don't need a university degree or some type of special educational certification to write a book and sometimes having such a distinction is not all that helpful. Many full time editors employed by large publishing houses can be a bit 'sniffy', sitting as they do, in under-heated second floor offices clutching their English Lit. BSc. in one hand ... and writing their fifth rejection slip of the day with the other. As long as *you* know who and what you are, that will genuinely be enough. You may feel you could get a kick start by *studying* and then by default, *copying* the style and language of other successful authors. Don't bother. Unless you are *that person*, you will never be able to write like *that person*. Just be yourself. You either want to write … or you don't. There are no short cuts! So, does your manuscript have 'style'? Well only you can decide that and if you want your work to be commercially successful, then you will need it in spades. Creating a 'style' of writing involves laying down the written word in a unique manner. It may be how you describe certain situations, the way you tell your story or the way you dress your characters. Style is a writer's finger print … and normally can't be copied well as proven by many ghost writers employed by some publishers to write under the name of already famous and established authors.

Tip 69: Are Sentences Concise?

As your manuscript is in effect a structured collection of sentences, it is important to understand what they do. They support and underpin your theme and they should say to the reader exactly what you mean to say. They can be short or long but my advice will always be … not *too* long, unless you are able to use the correct grammatical tools to stop your reader from getting out of breath. Sentences and their structure also create atmosphere and a short, concise delivery of them by your characters become particularly poignant when used in conversation.

Tip 70: Is Conversation Crisp?

One of the keystones of writing conversation must be to simply write as *you* speak, having conversations in your book that your character would have in real life. You have invented your characters, so it must be fairly straight forward to mimic their conversation. This will put a stamp of uniqueness and authority on your work, allowing you to stand out from other submissions littering the crowded editor's desk. As stated earlier, it will be to your advantage to avoid long, rambling paragraphs unless you have the grammatical skill to make the words flow correctly. The words you use and more importantly, the words you allow your characters to use, also dictate the tone of your writing and that tone translates to how the reader views your work, how involved he or she may become with your characters and most importantly, how they will react to the actions of your characters. Conversation is king!

Tip 71: Does It Flow?

When your characters are having a long and serious thought, it's a good idea to make sure it's actually part of the plot. It can be all too easy to fall in to the trap of giving out long and confusing thoughts that are not really related to the story line. The reality is, unless a beautifully crafted thought has some positive influence on the outcome of the current situation, then it stands the chance of diverting the reader's attention away from the action. If however, the 'musing' described as a 'thought' is important to the plot, make sure this adds to the tension of the moment rather than subtract from it. When you have changed an item of script from something that may impair the process of 'pace' and 'flow' to something that adds to it, you will find this pushes the reader forward, wanting to know if the involved character actually *did* have some sort of 'thrill'!

Tip 72: Does It Have Pace?

Just about every first manuscript for a work of fiction, produced by new or existing and experienced authors, will contain many words of description that are unnecessary. Good descriptions are really good and too many descriptive elements can be really bad. They slow down the pace, make the action long winded and often encourage the reader to 'put it down'! Describing people, happenings, events and scenarios is one of the corner-stones of good writing. However, there are some 'descriptive ways' that need watching, carefully. The rules are simply not to get weighed down with a particular situation that throws you into a position where you are scraping the barrel for more adjectives. Good pace is far more important to the success of your writing project than the ability to create descriptive sentences. Less is always more!

Tip 73: Is The Phrasing Good?

I was told many years ago by a professional writer who had been 'banging the keys' for a considerable number of years that the secret of good phrasing is making your sentences concise and ensuring your words link well. He was of course, absolutely right. Similes are often used to express a certain situation and lend some weight to a particular phrase. If you use similes, do so sparingly as it's just so easy to rely upon them to tell your story. Good phrasing is essential to good writing so make sure, in the edit, you have it under control. Phrases can also be a curse as well as a blessing. The curse is they often become addictive and as a result are simply used too much. The blessing is that you can of course create atmosphere and even a bit of humor with a sprinkling of good and correctly applied phrases. Where do they come from? They come from you writing them down as you hear or see them written. As a writer, you will be in continuous research for your current work or your next one and locking your mind on to the characters and situations around you on a daily basis enables you to recall them at a later date. Watch and listen and as you turn the next corner, you may hear the echoing words to be spoken by your very next villain or hero.

Tip 74: What About Word Choice?

I find it can be far too easy to be a bit too 'high brow' with word choice. The pace of your manuscript will be lost the first time your reader has to reach for the dictionary to find out what a particular word means. Use a Thesaurus to not only ensure you have a range of words available to you in your search to describe a particular situation, but also to sort words and place them in some preference of order. If you get stuck on a word, it's a good idea *not* to angst over it for hours or even minutes. Simply put the word 'blank' in the space you are looking to fill and go back to it later. Don't risk encountering the deadly disease of 'writers block' over the basic choice of ways to be 'superb' – such as … excellent, outstanding, wonderful, terrific, splendid, fabulous, fantastic, marvelous, magnificent, superlative, tremendous, brilliant, etc … etc.. Do you see what I mean? Using everyday words for everyday situations is normally a winner. However, be careful in too liberal a use what are deemed to be in current society … expletives or 'cuss' words. They can be very effective in the right place and can often be used effectively to reflect the 'reality' of a particular situation. However, they may be a 'curse' in their own right and my advice would be to ration them carefully.

Tip 75: Well Developed Characters?

This often discussed and relentlessly quoted subject is regularly linked to criticism rather than praise. An editor may refer to 'character development' in writing up his or her comments on your submitted manuscript, which is generally taken as 'editor-speak' for … 'have you done any?'

So, what is character development? Well, it's basically creating a character in your mind and then building up a complete life of the character as a series of notes or a full-blown mini life story. The subject has been touched upon earlier in Tip 09: Character Research Plan. The process of character development adds necessary depth and even some much needed life in to what may have slipped by unnoticed as a rather flat personality. As such, this character may end up being one that does not come over well within the twists and turns of the plot at the heart of your manuscript.

A good development process would be to start listing your characters life points; where they were born, went to school, went to university, first job, career path etc. Then you need to describe them, physically. If you know your characters well, and you will by the time you have finished an extensive character development project, then you can avoid falling into the less experienced author's trap of putting them in the wrong place at the wrong time or asking them to do things that are - for them – physically impossible. Again, it is worth remembering that if you write a full and detailed sketch of your story *before* you go to work on the real thing – as recommended – then developed character profiles will form part of that process.

There is much written about the art of forming and developing fictional characters and a quick search on the Internet may prove fruitful if you want to know more. For those of you who have been fortunate enough to have led a good life, travelled well and met lots of interesting people, you will no doubt be blessed with the ability to draw on such experiences when forming the characters for your work of fiction. However, if this is not the case then a great imagination and some study of the subject may serve you well.

Part 11:
The Edit

If you are a lonely, up in the attic or on the kitchen table EBook or self-published writer, then the odds are you will probably *not* have a professional editor working for you. They are available of course, for a fee and you will find many offering their services on the Internet. One recommendation I can make is AutoCrit, a very substantial editing tool that will take the guesswork out of the editing process. (See the detailed note at the end of this book). If you can afford it, buy the full blown version and I don't think you will regret it. However, if this option is not affordable, the manual editing of a final manuscript is an absolutely essential part of the publishing process and will be the deciding factor as to whether your labour of love and dedication is to be a success or failure. The 'self-edit' should not be undertaken the day after you place the final full stop. My advice would be to wait some time after the completion of your manuscript before tackling a full blown edit. You could also bear in mind that the editing function is not simply pushing your finished words through a spellchecker, although that is a fairly obvious operation to attend to early on in the editing process. Here are some things to think about.

******

Tip 76: Language – Spell Correction:

Perhaps you will have been spell checking as you go along. It's a good idea … and that's how I approach it. Even if you carry out an ongoing spell-check, it's a good idea to make sure you complete a double-check at the edit stage. Depending upon the market you're looking to sell your book into, and in particular the setting of the work, you have to decide whether your book is to be spell-checked in American English or British English. There is a substantial difference as in 'labor' and 'labour' or 'recognize' and 'recognise'. No matter what your feelings on the matter the simple answer to the problem is 'time'. If you are happy with American English then fire up the 'WP' spell-checker and off you go. If you wish to stick to the British way of doing things, then be prepared to update your spell-checker to accept the British English spelling and grammar. Spell checkers are sometime lacking in accuracy and scope, so make sure any words thrown up with an unacceptable correction resolution are run through a good quality dictionary. You won't regret it!

Tip 77: Grammar:

Grammar correction is always a problem area as anyone who went to school fifty years ago would simply not recognize what appears to be acceptable written grammar today. For example, I can tell you when I went to school, it would be an absolute sin to start a sentence with 'and' or 'but'. However, today, as instigated *for*, and popularized *by* lazy copy writers and journalist's, starting a sentence with 'and' and often with 'but' appears to be perfectly acceptable. There are the old favorites such as 'have got', 'you and me' instead of 'you and I' and 'earnt' instead of 'earned', so in effect, the field appears to be wide open for your own take on putting down the written word. Does it matter much? Probably not, as long as the reader isn't put off by what he or she may perceive as poor grammar. So it really depends upon your target market. If it's the younger person, then you can get away with more or less anything. If your audience is in a much older category, then grammar will need some detailed attention. The decision is finally yours … or in the event you are one of the lucky ones … your publisher!

Tip 78: Action Feasibility:

A vehicle, with a V8, 350 cu.inch engine travelling from New York to Chicago, non-stop on three gallons of fuel … is not feasible. A character diving into thirty feet of freezing cold water and swimming several miles in five minutes without surfacing for air …is not feasible. Being stopped with a shot in the chest, by a .45 caliber soft nosed bullet, at close range would not normally allow a character to then run three hundred yards in ten seconds, jump off a burning building and finally drive a car several miles to a hospital … it's not feasible. So, when in the final edit phase it really is advisable to look hard for some of those occasions where you may have been a little carried away with the action and allowed it to drift off in to the realms of fantasy … that is of course assuming you are not writing a fantasy story. If you are to produce fiction that has an historical setting but not fantasy, it's a good thing to make sure the action scenes hold on to some semblance of reality. Do the research and then you won't get caught out!

Tip 79: Character Feasibility:

No one knows your main character better than you! I have touched on this before and whether you appreciate it or not, a major part of the makeup of your main character is in fact …YOU! Your character will probably react to situations and scenarios the same way *you* would react. The real problem for you as the writer is it's often difficult to push the curtain aside and see that your personality is actually having an effect on a *written character* … who may look great to you … and your close family … but not so engaging to others who don't know you and therefore will be unable to make the association. This is a substantial pitfall and is avoided by ensuring you write a detailed sketch (yes … I labor the point yet again!) of the proposed novel and ask someone not that close to you to read it first and then give you an honest opinion. This will often lead to you consciously and forcefully changing the type, style and maybe even attitude of your main character, divorcing him or her from you completely. Instead of your new character reacting to a situation as you would actually react, you may find him or her making moves, decisions and actions that you, as an individual, would never dream of taking in a month of Sundays. As a result, you will be freed from the shackles of inadvertent character familiarity. Your writing could now become much more exciting … and you will possibly not be able to wait to 'get at it' every single day. Now you will be really and truly writing about someone else … NOT an opaque reflection of yourself! My advice would be to take this on-board. It will save much heartache later when the first person who reads your manuscript … who also knows you well … deliver's the words "It all seems to be about you!" This, quite frankly, is the very last thing you want to hear and maybe months of hard work has evaporated in the single moment you realize you have been writing a poorly disguised biography … and not a fiction thriller. The frightening thing is of course, everyone will be able to see it … except you! So, beware of making *you* the main character in your manuscript and try to make sure all your characters end up being describable, feasible, believable and engaging individuals with a life of their own.

Tip 80: Character Thoughts:

Again, I have touched on this earlier, but it's an important point to make. When your characters are having a long and serious thought about some situation or other and you are describing the thought process, it's essential to make sure this bit of writing is actually part of the plot. It's also important to make sure that 'thoughts' described in writing are indicated as actually being thoughts and not conversation. Again, you may smile at this observation but there are many books out there where you will have to work hard to define the difference. Unless the object of the thought has some important part to play in future chapters, why is your character thinking about it? The reality is that unless this beautifully crafted thought has some positive influence on the outcome of the current situation, then it stands the chance of diverting the reader's attention away from the action. My advice would be to make every effort to avoid switching and swapping thought for conversation, but if your character is on his or her own and in a tight situation, perhaps defining a particular line of thought will lead the scene through to a further, differing outcome than that expected by the reader. Finally, if the 'musing' described as a 'thought' is important to the plot, then it should be 'hard' edited to maintain pace and a solid connection with the story line.

Tip 81: Descriptive Opportunities:

It's generally true that just about every first manuscript for a novel, produced by new or existing and experienced authors, will contain many words of description that are unnecessary. As I may have intimated before "Good descriptions are really good and too many descriptive elements can be really bad". They slow down the pace, disrupt the flow and can make a lead in to the action long winded. A convoluted descriptive piece, if allowed to find its way through to the final manuscript, can often encourage the reader to 'drop it'! Describing things, people and events well is one of the corner-stones of writing. However, there are some 'descriptive ways' that need watching carefully. You are now at the 'edit' stage and will need to be ruthless in taking words out that are not required. The very best advice is to … 'grit your teeth and Just Do It!'

Tip 82: The Annoying Simile:

Yes, you will have noticed that they are everywhere and as I said earlier, you can read them in many books by other writer's ie *Slipping through his fingers like mercury'*.
You can hear them on TV. You can find them on posters. You can read them in newspapers and you

can hear them in everyday conversation. The way to capture these elusive phrases is to keep a record of them. The easy way to do it, of course, is to carry a piece of paper and a pen around with you and write them down. Other ways of recalling these little gems is to have a miniature tape recorder in your pocket, or in the car, and with most mobile phones' you can simply create an audible note and write down your Similes later. Again, we have talked about this process of recording information before. So you would be well advised to make sure you keep a master file of them all; you will be amazed at how quickly the file builds up.

The 'Analogy' and the 'Metaphor' need to be treated in the same way. Capture them wherever and whenever you hear or see them and build up your file - your secret weapon to be brought in to the line of attack when all seems lost. In the right place, such creative writing can be an asset to the finished work. The secret is not to have them lurking somewhere in every paragraph and whatever you do, try not to repeat any particular one when you have used it early on in a manuscript. Even with twenty chapters between Similes, your reader will instantly remember where he or she read the first one … and you, as the author, will receive a black mark!

Tip 83: Being Bold:

As you well know by now, if you have a publisher, then the more painful processes involved with an edit will be managed for you ... by others. However, as a self published writer, you are blessed with not having to listen to reasons why your book has been nearly cut in half at the whim of the editor's blue pencil. The reason is of course because this responsibility is now yours. So, you will have to steel yourself, and with the electronic equivalent of the infamous 'blue pencil', begin to take out 'unnecessary narrative'. I find one good way to do it is to let two or three people read the manuscript first and then ask them for an honest opinion about how they thought the book actually 'flowed'. Were they so enthralled, they could not put it down? If so, you must have it about right. Did they read it in several sessions but thought it was OK? Then you may have a problem with 'pace' and not being able to hold the reader's attention. This means you may have to undertake some heavy editing of script between actions and this will inevitably involve some re-writes. This is the point in your writing career when you need courage. A full and final edit is not for the faint hearted, so go to work with boldness and confidence. The real test will be when you read it back later. If you are happy with the result ... then this is a good result. If you are not, go back through the saved edited versions and see what may need putting back. You may find some little gems here you had little use for halfway through Chapter six. You have saved all the edits of course?

Tip 84: Throwing It Away?

One of the several, but not so obvious golden rules of fiction writing is to never throw any of your work away! No matter how hard you edit ... or let others edit for you, make sure you keep every word you extract or change from your original and very first manuscript. The most sensible way of editing is to start with the original manuscript file in a folder and name it 'Original'. Copy that folder and file and rename it 'First Edit'. Now you can start working on that file and when you have finished your first attempt at editing, shut down the file, saving the file within the 'First Edit' folder. Then save the folder and its file as 'Second Edit'. When you go back to the 'edit' process again, you will use this folder and file. After you finish your next edit session, carry out the same file saving action again so that you build up a selection of files you can find easily on your system, all at various states of editing. Why - do you ask - should a busy author have to go through such a tedious process and have loads of files hanging around an over-crowded laptop, ones that could possibly never be needed again? Well, sometimes the blue pencil can become a bit of a tyrant and suddenly, you may find that to achieve the status of a 'novel' for example, you may have to add a few words 'back' in to the manuscript … and if you've thrown them all away, or simply have such a screwed up filing system that you can't find them, then you have to get your writing head on and start filling in and padding out … all over again. A good edit should provide a crisp, exciting reading experience in a novel with pace and action right from the start. Remember the golden rule; you know exactly what is going to happen on each page … but your reader does not! Your cover 'Blurb' and great graphics may lure the reader in to buying the book, but a good edit will keep him or her turning the pages and looking out for your next one.

Tip 85: Employing An Editor:

This is a difficult one for no other reason than the sensible side of your brain will be telling you … 'Yes. I must employ an Editor for my manuscript' However, the practical side of your brain will be asking … 'Can I afford it?' The answer can be found possibly on the Internet and with the current easy electronic interchange of files, it doesn't really matter much where the service, or the individual providing the service, is located. A good and experienced editor can completely transform a 'not so snappy' piece of work into a best seller. A bad one can leave you bruised and hurt after hacking your manuscript to pieces until there is nothing recognizable of the original work left. The best advice is to get lots of quotes; ask for names of established writers who are their customers and most importantly, speak with them directly over the telephone, wherever they are. You will know in the first minute whether you can work happily together ... or not! Of course, if you have found yourself a Mentor who has connections in the publishing world, then he or she would be the first port of call. Recommendation means a lot where editors are concerned and a large degree of trust will be required between you and your chosen editor if both parties are to benefit from the relationship.

Tip 86: Finished?

Have you really finished your edit? Are you happy with the result? Do you feel confident enough to go to the next stage and actually get your work out there? If the answer is yes, then you can start thinking about preparing to put your finished work up for publishing. However, before you do, there is another old, but still golden rule for authors, which tells you ... at this stage, to put the manuscript away and not look at it for a month. This is not the first time I have said it ... and it will not be the last. When you have done that, take it out and read it again. If you still like it ... publish it. If you don't, go back to the sketch and a re-write. It will save you from a certain amount of disappointment and maybe some small measure of embarrassment!

Part 12:
The Cover

With a manuscript now ready to go, you have to think about the 'production' of your work. Probably the first thing to tackle is a cover … or jacket. If you are only self-publishing in EBook format, then you will need an eye catching cover image. If you are looking to produce your book in a paperback print format with a POD service, then you will need to equip yourself with a jacket that will 'wrap' round the book on three sides … front, back and spine.

******

Tip 87: What About A Cover?

As a self-publisher, there are three choices when considering providing your book with a cover. The first is to do it yourself; the second is to employ a designer of some description … and the third is to use the on-line facility provided by your chosen POD service provider. Whatever choice ou make, it's fairly essential that the cover image produces the right result. It will need to contain, or indicate to the reader, the key elements of your story. It will need to be eye-catching and look good as a full color image printed to your chosen book size as well as a thumb-nail against the title of your book on Amazon. One of the warning notices to take heed of is to ensure that any images used in putting together your cover graphic are royalty free or correctly purchased from the owner of the copyright.

Tip 88: Do It Yourself:

The 'do it yourself' option is not so daunting as it initially appears. You do not need to have ten years experience behind the baffling menu options in Photoshop to produce a startlingly good cover image. I do my own and do them for other people using a simple but very effective program from Serif Software called DrawPlus. You can look this software manufacturer up on the web and download the drawing software for free. You only need to get your head around the following few basics.

Page size: Whatever screen size you are working on, you will need to be able to set the scale of the printed page in inches or centimeters. It goes without saying that the bigger screen you have to work from, the better where high end graphics are concerned.

Importing images: You will need to master the ability to import an image on to the working page and then manipulate it in terms of size and position. This is normally a straight forward process using 'handles'.

Transparency: This is the single most useful tool

needed to 'blend' images together and with the 'arrange' tool, you can bring them to the front or send them to the back of the page. This, in effect, allows you to 'stack' images, one on top of the other.

Layers: This facility will allow you to work on your building image in various layers of control. By working in layers, you are able to manipulate an image in one particular layer without affecting the position of others in different layers. This is especially useful when putting down a background and overlaying images and script on top.

These are the key elements of a drawing program required to produce an exciting cover image, and with a bit of practice, you could well wonder why you ever thought of paying for a design. The operating functions are similar on most drawing software, so get to grips with the problem and save yourself a lot of money along the way. Take some time to 'play about' with the software. It won't bite back or crash and even if it does 'give up the ghost' on you due to some sort of mismanagement, you can simply reload the program and start again ... because it's FREE! You can find more detail relating to the 'elements' of a cover graphic later

Tip 89: Employ An Artist:

Employing an artist or designer is a route that many self-published authors are forced to tread. It's expensive (relatively) and you will need to give the individual involved a very concise and specific brief. An artist or designer will not keep submitting endless proofs to you, simply waiting for your approval. His or her time costs 'money' and so your brief had better be right first time out. Some will send you a form to fill in containing all the information they require to put together an initial image. Others may well want to discuss the project on the telephone supported by a detailed brief from you. Whatever your choice of designer, the golden rule is that if you find a good one, make sure you keep him (her)! Pay them on time; tell them you really like their work, give them a credit in your book and try to keep in touch between book projects. Finding a good graphic artist or designer who can come up with an eye catching cover graphic, sympathetic to your work … and someone you can have a proper conversation with is rare. When you do eventually find one, make sure you do not let them go! Your local newspaper is still the best place to find a graphic artist if you have no recommendations and of course, if all else fails, then there is the Internet. Of course, the obligatory word of warning must be 'do not part with loads of cash until you have seen some work'. A good and honest designer will come with one or two ideas against your brief before asking for large amounts of money. There is one final point to remember. You will inevitably be asked what 'resolution' you require for your final graphic, and this can vary depending upon who you will be submitting your final work to. However, the normal minimum standard is 300 dpi. The definition of dpi is as follows.

Dots per inch (DPI) - is a measure of spatial printing or dot density, in particular the number of individual dots that can be placed in a line within the span of 1 inch (2.54 cm).

KDP, for example, require 300 dpi or better and I normally provide them with a 450 dpi image to ensure good, clean edges to the title script. You can, in most cases, set the dpi value on many drawing programs when you export the final image into a drawing file type such as .jpeg or .gif. In others, you may need to set the DPI value in 'settings' before you start to set up your page.

Tip 90: Cover Elements:

There are three main elements involved in producing a cover. The first is the background, the second relates to the images used and overlaid on to the background, and the third is the script makeup and fonts used to be laid over the images and perhaps the blurb. So, in effect, you will be working with a minimum of three layers. The choice of background can be a final choice element of plain white or a block color that should not overpower the imported images.

If your work is a thriller, the background may move toward being a primary color but if you have produced a romantic novel then you will possibly need a more pastel shade … or simply no background color at all. If you are producing your own cover, you would be advised to set up a layer for each image used, so you can work on them individually without disturbing the setting of other images on the page. This is especially important when using images that have been altered using the transparency tool, as you will often need to move them about the page to see what level of blending is required with other images beneath the layer you are working on. Reading the help files of your chosen drawing program will resolve most issues relating to 'layering' as you tackle your cover project.

Tip 91: Image Elements:

In essence, the images on your cover should tell the story, grab the attention of the shelf scanning reader and be compatible with the accompanying 'blurb'. The blurb is a very condensed version of your final synopsis and will sit on the back cover of the jacket or sit alongside your thumbnail image in an on-line bookstore. If you are assembling your own images, please make sure they are *free* to use. Many images are available in good quality, high resolution for you to play with as long as they are not used simply on their own and must be 'worked' or 'manipulated' to meet the conditions of the license. An excellent facility to wander through on the internet is *morguefile.com* where you can find a great selection of images to download, mostly provided in acceptable resolutions. If you are attempting to put together your own cover, I cannot over emphasize that you make good use of the 'transparency' option in your drawing program. There is normally a wide range of effects to chose from that will blend your images together so that you end up with a professional looking cover plate. Also make use of the image 'crop' function to ensure you are only using that part of the image you need. Even if you are employing an artist or designer, it is often well worth sending him or her, a selection of images to give them an idea of what you have in mind to be included in the final production.

Tip 92: Technical Elements:

The technical aspects of producing a cover for your book project relate to the fact that it's a work of fiction. If you had been writing a non-fiction book about say the Architectural Heritage of the Pentagon, it would be fairly easy to put a picture of the Pentagon building on the front cover and everyone looking at it on the bookshelf will quickly gain an idea about the contents. It would therefore be great if the cover of your book gave the potential reader a similar insight. There are no golden rules here except to say look at lots of covers on the Internet and see which ones leap out of the screen for you. You may like the simple image such as a knife with blood dripping from it, the shadowy face of a wild eyed man or shocked and frightened woman. If you have a friend with a good resolution camera or camera-phone, invite them over to take some pictures using yourself as a model making sure you have hung a bed sheet, or something similar, over a door to create a neutral background for your image. This will allow you to 'cut out' the image from the background in your drawing program. You can do the same with 'props' of course using the bed sheet on a table for the neutral background requirement. If you are keen to use multiple images to tell the story, it's a good idea to make sure your final image is not overcrowded. Less is much, much more here! When overlaying script, it's also good practice to check that the font you use is legible, not only displayed on a full size cover but also as a thumbnail image on the Internet. Having a great image, but not being able to read the title and the name of the author is not recommended.

Tip 93: Cover Importance:

There is no doubt that a good cover image is one of the really important things to get right when producing your finished work. It's the first thing your potential reader will be drawn to whether buying your book in hard copy from a bookshop or as an electronic edition on the Internet. It should firstly be eye-catching and secondly indicate what could be between the pages at a glance. This is of course a substantial target to aim for but a good cover image or jacket *will* sell your book … of that, there is no doubt. Whether you will be able to produce a cover yourself, that is commercial and professional looking, or be inclined to put a brief out to an artist or designer, *you* should be happy with the end result before publishing. No one knows what is between the covers of your book … except you! Therefore, the cover is in fact a full color invitation to a potential reader to flip it open and start to absorb the words. If they then like the sample, they almost inevitably buy. If your cover is not able to entice a potential and curious reader to 'find out more'… then it's possible you will simply not sell it!

Part 13:
The Blurb

The dictionary definition of 'blurb' is as follows; "A promotional description, as found on the jackets of books..." So, now we know what a 'blurb' is, we need to know where it comes from and what disguises it may appear in. The 'blurb' is as important to your finished book promotion as the cover. However, it's often seen as technically difficult to distil the storyline of a 70 to 120 thousand word work of fiction into a couple of explosive lines of 'promotional description' or one, single electrically charged paragraph. Read on!

******

Tip 94: The Synopsis:

This is where it all starts. The synopsis is simply a distillation of the 'sketch' ... and the 'blurb' is equally a distillation of the synopsis. Therefore, the quality of your sketch and the closeness of it to your finished work will provide you with the ideal platform from which you can start the 'distillation' process. A synopsis will usually be a short document of one, or not much more than two A4/Letter size pages with standard line spacing. Your sketch may well be anything from ten to thirty pages, so this is where your work begins. It sounds impossible at first glance but tackled in a methodical way will soon provide the required result.

Here's how I do it. Take a copy of your sketch and highlight all the sentences that refer directly to the plot and storyline. These stay in. Now start taking out, sentence by sentence, all areas of script that do not refer directly to the plot or storyline. You will, at the end of this process have possibly reduced the sketch by half. Now undo the highlighting and start the process again until you end up with a synopsis. What will happen during this 'edit' is that as you look longer and longer at a page full of words, your brain will overtake your reluctance to take any away until it all becomes one fairly straightforward exercise. You can of course allow a professional editor to hack away at your work and come up with what they regard as a suitably lively and commercial synopsis. The risks involved in employing an editor are really only connected to your pride and the size of your bank account ... so weigh up the 'pros and cons' of doing it before committing to spending money on something you as a writer will, at some stage of your writing career, need to get your head round!

Tip 95: The Full Blurb:

The 'full' blurb, being a distillation of the synopsis, will by necessity end up as a quite intense description of the action taking place in your manuscript and a much condensed view of the key characters. With a synopsis weighing in at a full page or two, a full blurb will be less than a page and possibly no more than half a page. Ideally, it will be the right size to fill the rear of the cover jacket if you are producing for print. It will need to be punchy, truthful (no embellishments of people or situations that are not actually contained within the manuscript) and descriptive, providing tension and delivering the obvious question of 'what happens next?' Here's an example from one of my books – Rosalind.

When a stunningly beautiful, sexually aware woman and escape from a violent, abusive father combine with a new life in the big city, they make the story of Rosalind one of strength and determination in a quest to conquer her past.

A change of name completes her transformation in to a new woman, one who is swept off her feet by a handsome, staggeringly rich Arab Prince. But being isolated and then imprisoned in a desert Sheikdom, forced in to sexual slavery and foiled in her attempt to escape, leads to unexpected violence and a possible cover-up.

Her friend in New York is distraught and vows to confront the powerful, diplomatically protected Arab multi millionaire to get at the truth.

The ultimate encounter between one frighteningly resolute woman and the politically protected, influential, Arab Prince leaves a scene of carnage, as in the final account, only one person can walk away. But will there be more than one survivor, and who could it possibly be?

Set in the world financial depression of the 1970's, this is the sometimes heartbreaking story of powerfully portrayed characters that will become more and more a part of you with every turn of the page.

This full blurb is 200 words long and is divided into four paragraphs. The first three indicate the beginning, middle and end of the story and the final paragraph defines the setting of the story and a hint at the characterization involved.

Tip 96: The Short Blurb:

The 'short' blurb is a further distillation of the full blurb and will need to sum up the plot and main characters in short, explosive sentences. Here's an example taken from the descriptive information contained in the 'long blurb' above.

Its 1970's America and a quest for sexual fulfillment leads Rosalind into the clutches of a deceitful Arab Prince. Forced into degrading sexual slavery in the overheated climate of a distant desert Sheikdom, could this be the end?

However, justice must be done in this powerful thriller, about strong women in a tough man's world of unbelievable riches and privilege, where survival is the only goal.

This short blurb has taken the complete synopsis from maybe 800 words down to the full blurb of 200 words and now 66 words. Finally, below is an even shorter 34 word single sentence blurb for the same storyline.

The deceiving affections of an Arabian Prince, sexual slavery, and a disturbing retribution: from the very start, two strong female characters are brought vibrantly alive in this thriller with a twist in the tail.

Tip 97: Blurb Importance:

The combination of 'blurb' and 'cover image' are at the heart of how successfully you will be able to market your book to potential readers. In effect, the blurb is the key element of tempting your reader to open the very first page. The cover image is designed to attract attention, but it is the blurb that actually advertises to the reader, what might be between the covers. There is a popular saying in the world of commercial advertising that goes like this.

"Good advertising can clear shelves; great advertising can build factories ..!"

So, you need to spend some time on getting your 'blurb' right ... it is your single 'advertising' opportunity at your point of sale. Distill with care making sure the key elements of your story remain after a final fierce edit. Get some other opinions on your final blurb. Ask friends to read it and tell you honestly if such a 'hook' would persuade them to buy the actual product.

Part 14:
What Next?

Having now produced your final manuscript, turned it into a book by adding a cover image or jacket and finally put together a hot blurb, you now need to get your 'product' in front or as many people as possible. There are lots of detailed actions you can take locally to bring attention to your work. There is of course much advice available on the Internet and many businesses offering to promote your book for you. However, no matter how eye catching the headline emphasizing the word 'FREE' … from my experience, there is not much out there that's really free

******

Tip 98: What Will You Do With It?

The big question facing all authors or novelists, new or old, is what to do next. You will of course need to technically put it all together to become a sellable product. There are many avenues to pursue on the Internet if you do not have an agent or traditional publisher. If you are not one of the fortunate few who will find a publishing deal somewhere, then you will need to go through all the processes described previously to arrive at this point which is a completed manuscript, fully edited and fit for uploading to the Internet. To accompany this work, you will need a cover image and/or jacket cover in a suitable electronic format to upload to the internet and a blurb to define your work in a particular genre. So that's it then!

Well before you jump one step forward, let's just check on 'what you going to do with it' and how you will go about doing it.

You will need to choose a vehicle enabling you to publish your book online in either one or both generally accepted formats – EBook and Print On Demand Paperback (PODP). There is little doubt that Amazon (EBook) and their wholly owned PODP publisher KDP, have a head start in most countries. As long as you have the right file formats to hand, uploading your material to either website is straight forward with lots of help along the way. There are or course many other service providers for self-publishing such as Lulu, Booktango, Smashwords, Booksie, Authorconnect, Bubok and many others. The process is much the same as with Amazon ie you upload a suitable word processing or .pdf file containing your manuscript followed by a cover image and finally a synopsis, a blurb and a bio of you, the author. You may have to wait some hours before you can see your finished work online, but in general the whole procedure is fairly straight forward. You will of course need to know your way around a computer and be reasonably efficient at file management. Other than that, you will be up and running in less than an hour and visible to the world within twenty four.

One important point to remember is that in the process of loading up your book to an on-line publishing service such as Amazon, you will also be allowed to provide yourself with an Author profile giving you a personal presence on the Internet. For Amazon, this is called Author Central. Once activated by you, it will give you a searchable presence on the Internet providing a wealth of information about you and your book or books. To start getting your name out and about on the Internet as an author, you will no doubt need to register with several websites who can usefully promote you as an individual. To do this effectively, you will need a good quality photo of yourself ... hopefully a 'true likeness' and ... for the more mature amongst you ... not one taken when you were in the first flush of youth. Get yourself a 'crisp' Bio together as a word document so you are uploading the same information to each site you register with. After a few weeks of being registered to some of the web sites you have chosen, put your name into a search engine and see what results you get. Then add the word 'author' to your name and search again. If you can fill the first three pages of results with sites that link to you in one way or another, then you will have manufactured the right result. There is of course, one word of warning. Whatever you do, and whoever you sign up with on-line, do *not* give away your rights. You should maintain the world wide publishing rights to your book under all circumstances. If you have a publisher, the negotiation of rights will part of your contract with them and probably linked to any advance payment offered. Again, be careful here and make sure you find yourself an agent to look after your interests. I know this costs money in terms of commissions, but better to pay a small sum in commissions than inadvertently give away the rights to your book … forever!

Tip 99: How Will You Sell It?

Now you are at the stage where your book is finished, a cover completed that you are happy with and all your files uploaded to an on-line publishing service. So, the next requirement is to actually 'sell it'!

You will not need a degree in marketing to organize the promotion and sale of your new book. Most on-line publishers will have a set of marketing tools available to you, as their customer, varying in cost from completely free to hundreds of dollars. If you have a budget for promoting your book, consider carefully the paying options each publisher will offer. If you have a convincing budget, you may find yourself leaning toward the many companies on-line who offer a 'paid for publishing' service where some guarantees are even provided assuring you of substantial sales through their own distribution network. Unless you have a particular reason for using such a service and don't really care how much you spend, my advice would always be to 'do it yourself' and spend your budget in areas of marketing that you have direct control over.

There are three differing activities requiring attention when planning to sell your book. The first is selling it in the original written language as an EBook or POD Paperback, which in this hypothetical case is English. The second is selling your book in other languages and the third is selling your work as an Audio Book.

Selling the EBook/Paperback Version. As intimated previously, there are many facilities available on the Internet to help you sell an EBook. If you have produced your book through Amazon in their Kindle format you will have the resources of a massive on-line business at your fingertips and it costs you … nothing! You can put your book on free promotion for up to five days at a time. I do this regularly, especially if one particular title starts to fall off in sales. This service is available under the KDP Select option. Your account with KDP provides an excellent set of reports showing book sales and your earnings. Your English language book will be sold through Amazon platforms in twelve countries, can be enrolled in a lending library for which you get paid and a countdown deal to link your EBook with a paperback version. There is also Author Central available that will automatically link to all your titles. In short, the whole Amazon experience for self published authors is probably the most comprehensive out there … and it's getting better! If you are able to combine your paperback publishing requirements with your EBook ambitions, then using KDP for both can be a winning combination. I hasten to emphasize the fact that there are many other platforms available to the self-published author, but from my experience, the overall package offered by Amazon is pretty hard to beat … and it's all FREE!

Selling your book in other Languages. There are unfortunately not many options here unless you are able to latch on to an agent who specializes in this kind of work. If you become a number one best seller on Amazon, they will of course be knocking your door down … so this could possibly be your initial aim. There is one operation out there on the web current at time of writing and it's called PubMatch.com. It's basically a shop window for authors and agents to see what's out there in terms of options. It describes itself as a 'Book Rights Network' facility and does what it says on the tin. There are Book Rights agents available who will only handle work that's already been published in its original language; so make sure you read any information provided to you via a website to ensure you qualify for a response. Like most traditional publishers and agents, you will be lucky to get any form of reply to your submissions unless you have written a blockbuster.

Creating an Audio Book. One other and very meaningful way to sell your work, and earn a financial return is to convert it into an Audio Book. If you live in the United States, then Amazon can provide you with a great facility through its wholly owned audio book producing business called ACX.com. The process is necessarily detailed, absolutely unique and well explained. What's on offer is quite a step forward in the Audio Book world and to grasp the full implications, you will need to visit the website. If you are published with KDP, there is a link on the home/sign in page. (Correct at time of writing) For the rest of us, I'm afraid the options are not too prolific. If you have the technology on your computer you can record your own audio book. If you are short on software there is an excellent free audio mixing program available on the Internet called

'Audacity' and once you know your way around it and equipped with a decent quality microphone, you can produce a more than acceptable file to upload to your on-line publisher. One small tip would be to listen to a few audio book samples first to get an idea how the file is formed in terms of announcing chapter changes etc.

Tip 100: Who Will Buy It?

The reading public can only feast their eyes on your latest offering if and when they know it is 'out there'! So, what are the options?

Social Media. As the biggest single market for book sales is now connected to the Internet in one way or another, you would be well advised to establish a presence there. You will need a website or a blog as a focus point for all your promotions to refer back to. A Blog such as WordPress, is normally totally free unless you want to register a domain name as your title ie. www.yourname.com. If you go for a website, you will still need a domain name and someone to host it. You can get good quality, free webhosting with no ads on the page from www.000webhost.com. You will of course require some knowledge of transferring files via FTP and a suitable FTP program. The world favorite right now is Filezilla … and it's FREE! There is of course a plethora of social media sites available to the hungry author including

Facebook and Twitter. Maintaining a presence on SM sites does take time, on a regular basis, but many a new author has been discovered on Facebook for example and these sites are followed worldwide. It's a good idea to think carefully about your target market when setting up the kind of individuals you want to connect with and respond to your tweets or postings.

Book Promotion Websites. As I said earlier, getting a web presence out there able to fill several pages on Google when anyone searches your name is the very best thing you can do, without it costing you any money. There are some good promotional services available and sites like GoodReads.com and AuthorsDen.com spring to mind. By registering on such sites and uploading your required data will normally generate a search result on the major search engines. So linking you to your published work on the Internet is achieved simply by using the facilities provided by these promotional sites.

Book Marketing. Unless you have some professional contacts able to assist in marketing your book, you will need to rely upon your own abilities and the services of websites such as AskDavid.com and SmashWords.com. However, local marketing of your work is just as important as getting your name out there on the Internet. It's a great idea to explore 'close by' avenues such as local radio and TV, talks to local societies and meeting groups, taking an 'ad' in local newspapers and handing out flyers in the nearest shopping mall. Get yourself some eye catching visiting/business cars printed from someone like on-line supplier 'Vistaprint' who can provide excellent quality at a very cost effective price.

Marketing is not a secret science; it's simply working in a structured direction to get as many people as possible to know about you and your book or books.

If you haven't done so already, create a monthly news letter and tell people something about your books and book projects or something interesting about you each month to keep your name in the front of their mind. You can make a 'subscribe form' to the newsletter available on your website and this way you will harvest email addresses of people who are in effect your unique audience. Don't forget to use your existing email address book and make sure you add a 'signature' at the bottom of all your outgoing mail with a promotional note for your book and a link back to your website or blog.

Sales Gimmicks. If you have a creative spirit, there are some opportunities to make book sales using a 'Gimmick' associated with your book. Successful past programs of this type have involved putting up a prize for hunting down a treasure using hidden clues contained within the storyline of the book. This type of promotion is financed by people buying the book at a premium price and registering on a website. It has made one or two people millionaires, but there are financial risks attached and care is advised.

Another Gimmick is to provide your book with more than one ending and ask readers to tell you which they prefer by voting through a website. The final vote then decides which ending will be used for the actual publication. It's all free to the participant but you will harvest a set of email addresses you can then use in email promotional campaigns.

You can spend a bit of time recording an interview with yourself if you have the means, ie a good quality video camera, and a patient friend or parent to do the interviewing. Script it out thoroughly giving an insight in to yourself as a writer and a description of the characters in the book. Make it about half an hour long and not too serious as your readers want to enjoy seeing it, and raising a smile now and again is good PR. The gimmick is to offer this interview as perhaps a CD to readers of your book or as an online link on your website to a page where potential viewers will need to enter their email address to see it. Again, you benefit from harvesting the email addresses and using them in future promotions.

The Process. The whole process of 'What Next' after you have written your novel is one of choice. The old saying of 'The harder I work, the luckier I get!' must have been written for writers of fiction, but bear in mind the rewards can be great, not only in terms of satisfaction but financially too. There will be many of you who only want to write to actually achieve a particular goal and others who want to be 'rich and famous'… but whichever path you tread and possibly several paths between, it's worth remembering that only *you* can make the process enjoyable and only *you* can make it a personal disaster. This is not about teamwork … it's about you, creativity and discipline. The process of selling and marketing your work will take as long and as much dedication as was required to write it in the first place. This is often forgotten in the rush to get words down on paper. So, when you have finished writing and then marketing your novel or great book of fiction, you should sit back and congratulate yourself for a job well done!

101: Did You Enjoy It?

A time for reflection perhaps? If you really did enjoy the experience of writing your work of fiction, then you will possibly want to do it all again. My advice would be not to rush in to it until you are satisfied with the results of your first one ie sales, promotion results, feedback from reviews, feedback from friends and the fact of whether you have the likelihood of making any money or not! Much is learnt in the process of writing a book, most of which will be an understanding of what suits *you* best. The way you go about it and the result you get will be totally of your doing. Your confidence in yourself, your dedication to the project and your determination to succeed will combine to produce a finished and 'polished' result. Writing should not be a chore … it should be an enjoyable experience with a complete adrenalin rush at the very end when you view your written word in print with an astounding cover you designed and constructed yourself. So finally, let's quickly go over what I consider to be the most important points of this little book of 'tips' for the fiction writer.

Being Organized. Be organized before you start, allowing you to plan to succeed rather than by default … planning to fail.

Your Subject. Choose it carefully and know it well. This will ensure you do not 'run out of steam' around fifty pages in. If you know your subject well, the words will flow.

Have a Plan. If you don't have a plan, you could end up being the victim of time management. Don't let that happen to *you*.

Produce a Sketch. Many of you may not want to go

this route, but my advice would be if you are unsure in any way about the 'length and breadth' of your story … write a sketch!

Setting up the Manuscript. You will encounter less formatting problems at the end of your project by setting up the page on your WP software from the very beginning. If you are looking to produce a paperback with your work, then my best advice is to set up the manuscript document for print with correct gutters, mirror margins and page numbers to the book size you feel appropriate.

The Diseases. Remember that writer's diseases are contracted by you and only you can control the recovery. Tackle self-doubt head on and simply 'do not give up'.

A Mean Edit. Yes … you really do have to be mean to yourself in the edit process. It is the singular most important part of the process of writing good fiction. My advice would be *not* to underestimate what's involved and ensure that when you've finished you will hold in your hand a lean and athletic version of your story, one that has legs and will take you all the way to the finishing line.

The Cover. This is all about your creative ability, the experience you may or may not have with simple drawing programs, and absolute confidence. If you feel that producing a good cover or jacket is beyond you, for whatever reason, then invest in a good artist or designer and try to establish a relationship with them … if you find a good one. They are generally very rare!

Promoting Your Book. There are many avenues to stroll down in a search for the very best way to promote your finally produced book. Unfortunately, there are no set formulae for success but I have covered one or two ideas you might try within the pages of this book of tips. There are many more ideas and services on offer out there and the Internet is of course a mine of information. My advice, as always is, why pay for something when you can get it for free. So, beware of those service providers who purport to be FREE … when in fact what they offer for FREE will not do 'what it says on the tin' … and is simply there to suck you into parting with some money.

******

Finally, if you have now been through the process of writing fiction, for fun or for profit, and didn't really enjoy it … you may need to start at Part One again. If, however you found the whole experience exhilarating and fulfilling, then there is one last little tip I can give you.

REVIEWS: When your readers begin to take up your book, there are many who will write reviews. Some make a profession of being critical, therefore some may be good ... and some may be bad. Take my advice: feed off the good ones and simply ignore the bad ones. If they were all so damned good out there, they would be doing it themselves!

******

NOTE: In Part 11, The Edit, we mention a piece of software (or App if you prefer) designed specifically as a comparative editor for writers of all types and genres. It is easy to use although complex in nature and works on a simple number rating system of 0 to 100 to rate your work. If you can end up with a rating of 90+ for your manuscript, then you will be doing very well, and in the reporting process, if you correct all the highlighted queries, there will be NO mistakes or missed errors. The on-board algorithms apply a wide selection of standards against which to evaluate your work supplying you with the ability to compare your text against the all-inclusive set of genre descriptions as listed below.

AutoCrit Genre - Compare Your Text

General Fiction, Non-Fiction Narrative, Non-Fiction Prescriptive, Academic, Biography & Memoir, Business, Fantasy, Health & Wellness, Historical Fiction, Horror, Magazine, Movie Script, Mystery & Suspense, Newspaper, Political, Romance, Science Fiction, Sci-Fi & Fantasy, Short Story, Spiritual, Young Adult.

There is also the option to compare the text of your uploaded manuscript to a particular style of writing, as linked to the comprehensive list of International authors below. If this list of top International authors does not excite you as an aspiring or growing author, then stick with the genre option.

AutoCrit Authors – Compare Your Text

Adam Gopnik, Adam Nevill, Ann Rice,Barbara O'Neal, Beverly Jenkins, Brandon Sanderson, Brenda Jackson, Brene Brown, Bran Keene, Dale Carnegie, Dan Brown, Dan S Kennedy, Dan Simmons, Daniel, H Pink, Daniel Silva, Danielle Steel, Dean Koontz, Debbie Macomber, Deepak Chora, Diana Gabaldon, Don Miguel Ruiz, Emily Giffin, Eoin Colfer, George R.R. Martin, Gore Vidal, Graham Hancock, Henry Kissinger, Hilary Mantel, Issac Asimov, J.K. Rowling, J.R.R. Tolkien, James Herbert, James Patterson, James S.A. Corey, Jane Green, Jean Grainger, Jeannette Walls, Jeffrey Archer, Jennifer Weiner, Jerry B. Jenkins, Jodi Picoult, John Grisham, Jon Krakauer, Karin Slaughter, Kathy Reichs, Ken Follett, L.E. Modesitt, Jr., Lee Child, Madeleine L'Engle, Michael Connelly, Michael Crichton, Neil deGrasse Tyson, Nicholas Sparks, Orson Scott Card, Patricia Briggs, Philippa Gregory, Preston & Child, Ramsey Campbell, Richard Dawkins, Richard Laymon, Rick Riordan, Robert Greene, Robert Jordan, Robert T. Kiyosaki, Robyn Carr, Sam Harris, Sara J. Maas, Seth Godin, Sharyn McCrumb, Stephen Hawking, Stephen King, Stephen R. Covey, Suzanne Collins, Timothy Ferriss, Tom Clancy, Tony Robbins, Ursula K. Le Guin, Victoria Aveyard, Walter Isaacson, Zig Ziglar

Finally, there is little doubt the reporting structure of AutoCrit is probably beyond normal comparison. The broad depth and attention to detail in the reporting process offers the writer a certain level of assurance. The analysis of work is contained in over 30 individual reports as well as a master report showing overall results in graphic detail. Corrections are able to be made to any part of the manuscript at any time to create a new report and check your work as you progress.

AutoCrit Reports – Analyse your Text

Summary Report:
Pacing & Momentum Report:
Sentence Variation, Pacing, Paragraph Variation, Chapter Variation
Dialogue Report:
Dialogue Tags, Adverbs in Dialogue
Strong Writing Report:
Adverbs, Passive Indicators, Tense Consistency, Showing vs Telling, Cliches, Redundancies, Unnecessary Filler Words
Word Choice Report:
Initial Pronoun and Names, Sentence Starters, POV Consistency, Generic Descriptions, Homonyms, Personal Words and Phrases
Repetition Report:
Repeated Words, Repeated Uncommon Words, Repeated Phrases, Word Frequency, Phrase Frequency
Combination Report:
Overused Words, Combination Report
Readability Report:
Readability Statistics, Dale Chall Readability, Complex Words, Uncommon Words in Fiction
Grammar Report:
Spelling and Grammar

AutoCrit can never replace a collection of bright, professional (human) editors. However, it can replace the bill of several hundreds of pounds or dollars that come with such (human) services … and even then, you must expect there to be missed items and the odd spelling mistake here and there.

THE END
www.quentincope.co.uk

MECURIAN BOOKS

https://mecurianbooks.webnode.com